Unrestrained

Unrestrained

The Power of Praying without Limitations

Jason McKinnies

Unrestrained
The Power of Praying Without Limitations

Copyright © 2024 Jason McKinnies
First Edition
Nonfiction, Inspirational, Devotional

All rights reserved. No part of this publication may be reproduced, stored in a retrieval system, or transmitted in any form or by any means, electronic, mechanical, photocopying, recording, or otherwise without the prior written permission of the author. Reviewers may quote briefly for review purposes.

Scripture quotations are taken from the Holy Bible, New Living Translation (NLT), Copyright 1996. Used by permission of Tyndale House Publishers, Inc. Carol Stream, IL USA. All rights reserved.

Scripture quotations marked "NKJV" are taken from the New King James version. Copyright 1982. Used by Thomas Nelson, Inc. Used by permission. All rights reserved.

ISBN 979-8-9915684-0-1

Edited by Shelley Wilburn, Walking Healed Ministries and Mountain Joy Publishing
Cover Art by Paul Ruane
Graphics by Gordon Johnson from Pixabay.com

Published by Purpose House Publishing

Published in the United States of America

Table of Contents

Dedication i
Foreword ii
Introduction v
1 Abraham Prays Over Sodom 1
2 Jacob's Prayer for Mercy 5
3 Moses Prays to Overcome Doubt 9
4 Signs of the LORD's Power 20
5 When Prayer Turns to Praise 26
6 A Prayer of Intervention 31
7 Moses' Prayer of Repentance 35
8 Praying for God's Presence 40
9 A Prayer During Discouragement 46
10 A Prayer Against Rebellion 52
11 A 40-Day Prayer 57
12 Prayer After a Defeat 61
13 Praying for a Child 66
14 A Prayer of Praise 72
15 A Kingdom Minded Prayer 76
16 Praising for Deliverance 81
17 Praying for Wisdom 85
18 A Prayer of Dedication 90

19	A Prayer of Dejection	95
20	A Prayer Out of Distress	100
21	A Prayer for Healing	104
22	A Prayer of Thankfulness	108
23	A Prayer for Cheerfulness in Giving	112
24	A Prayer Motivated by Fear	117
25	Praying for a Nation	123
26	Begin with Prayer	130
27	Praying When Life Gets Overwhelming	135
28	Turning Your Prayer into Praise	140
29	A Prayer for a Clean Heart	146
30	The 23rd Psalm	151
31	A Prayer of Forgiveness	155
32	A Prayer for Guidance and Understanding	160
33	A Prayer for His Presence	166
34	A Prayer for Clarification	170
35	A Prayer to Not Miss Our Moment	175
36	A Prayer of Desperation	180
37	Our Prayer	185
38	I Pray for You	189
39	Praying Bold Prayers	194
40	Praying for Those Who are Doing Well	198
41	Pray Without Ceasing	203

42 A Prayer to be Sent..............................206

About the Author......................................220

Dedication

I dedicate this book to the people of Purpose House Church, who have believed, prayed, and lived for God without restraint. I sincerely appreciate that the people of Purpose House dedicate and consecrate twenty-one days to prayer each January. It is, and has been, the basis from which everything at Purpose House flows: prayer!

Foreword

I was walking out of church after services one morning and noticed my pastor, Jason McKinnies, walking toward me.

"Want to write a book on prayer?"

I answered with a resounding, "YES!"

Little did we both know the journey we were about to embark. A lot of struggles ensued. A pandemic, quarantine, illness, loss, surgery (mine), writing, re-writing, and re-writing. Also, computer problems, computers crashing, and manuscripts being lost. This was certainly a time of learning to pray bold and unrestrained prayers.

Prayer is something many people love to do, while others avoid like the plague. I believe we avoid it because we either don't know what to say, or we feel unworthy to approach our loving and merciful Father, God. Still, maybe we just feel as if we need to clean ourselves up before we can even think to ask God for anything. How untrue and devastating are these thoughts!

Throughout Scripture we are encouraged, no, commanded to come to God boldly and without restraint. We have permission to tell Him *everything* (Psalm 142).

This is why *Unrestrained* is such a wonderful book chock full of God's Word and prayers of saints of old. It instructs us to bring everything we have before the throne of God and receive His grace, mercy and forgiveness.

In *Unrestrained* you, the reader, will learn exactly how God wants you to come. Unrestrained means without restraint, with no ties holding you back. Nothing should keep you from praying to God; from pouring out your heart and soul, down to the most seemingly minute concern – all to a God who loves you so deeply that He sacrificed His only Son on a brutal cross, making Him the sin of all people (including you and me). He did this because He loves us so much and wants a close and beautiful relationship with those of us who would trust and love Him with our whole heart, soul, mind, and strength.

Jason does a wonderful job of bringing the Word to life, then expounding on the magnificent ways God used His people throughout Scripture to show us how to pray unrestrained prayers. *Unrestrained* is more than just a book of devotions. Inside these pages you will find God-breathed Scriptures which will speak deep into your heart and soul. Use them to begin your journey of praying unrestrained. Get bold. Read them out loud.

Use this book to dig deeper into God's Word for yourself to find the loving, merciful Father who loves *you* without restraint. The enemy of your soul has been stealing from you long enough. It's time to wake up and stand up, boldly declaring who and Whose you are!

Do it unrestrained!

"May the LORD bless you and protect you. May the LORD smile on you and be gracious to you. May the LORD show you his favor and give you his peace," ~*Numbers 6:24-26 (NLT).*

Shelley Wilburn
Writer, Author, Editor, Speaker, and Minister
Founder of Walking Healed Ministries
and Mountain Joy Publishing

Introduction

Unrestrained.

My favorite book of the Bible has always been the book of Acts. Quite simply, it is the one book of the Bible that is still being played out. It was titled the Acts of the Apostles, written by Luke, as a witness to the power that released into the believers of Jesus Christ.

One of the most exciting stories happened in Acts chapter three. There, Peter and John were on their way to pray. Upon coming to the Temple to pray, they encountered a lame man who was lame from when his mother gave birth to him. Every day this man was brought and laid by the gate called Beautiful. They carried the lame man to the gate daily to beg for money from those coming to the Temple.

Peter and John encounter this man lying by the gate called Beautiful. He does what he has always done, and they likewise were doing what they had always done. He asked for alms daily and they were following the custom of daily prayer. The difference on this day was made possible because of what happened in Acts 2, which was fulfilling the promise of Acts chapter one.

Previously, they went to pray, and it was the custom; customs are powerless. On the other hand, prayer combined with faith in Almighty God is powerful! Now, these men had been filled with the promise of power that Jesus said they would receive in Acts 1:5-8. On this day, they are headed to pray. Before they even get to pray, they break the custom, and the man who was laid by the gate called Beautiful is healed.

It always struck me that if Jesus likewise followed the custom and went to the Temple to pray, wouldn't He have also passed this man at this same gate? Why then, didn't Jesus heal him? The gate called Beautiful isn't listed as one of the gates into the city of Jerusalem in the book of Nehemiah; there must be something about this gate. Indeed, there is!

The word used in Scripture for beautiful has two definitions. One is the idea of being attractive, beautiful. The second definition for the word is for an opportune point of time. Indeed, the day that Peter and John were on their way to pray was the opportune time. It was the right time for this man's healing. His healing would catapult the message of Jesus, allowing people to hear the fantastic news of Jesus through the healing that happened at the gate called Beautiful.

When customs are broken and power is released outside of the normal channels of power and authority, you can be sure that there will be resistance. This case was no different.

Soon after the healing, the Apostles preached in what was called Solomon's Portico. Peter and John are talking with the people; men were sent to arrest them. Not everyone views miracles and the power of God as beautiful. God's power on display is considered to be a threat to the establishment. Just that short testimony of what happened at the gate and why it was possible because of the sacrifice of Jesus on the Cross of Calvary, five thousand people believed.

The apostles were threatened and then let go. What they do next is what they were going to the Temple to do in the first place, pray!

This prayer is a request for boldness. You would think after being arrested, threatened, and being forbidden to speak or preach the name of Jesus; the prayer would be for protection. Instead of asking for protection, they ask for more boldness!

Their prayer is a prayer we must pray! As the world spirals out of control, we, the people of God, must be bold. The Scripture records precisely what happened when they prayed; not after or before, rather when and while they prayed, the place was shaken. That is what we need across the aisles, across our streets, and around the world: a spiritual shaking that brings about an awakening.

The Scripture records that after the shaking, they were all filled with Holy Spirit, and they spoke the Word of God with boldness. The Passion Translation (TPT) states that they spoke the Word of God *unrestrained*. They received the power to believe, preach, teach, pray, and declare the word without restraint.

My prayer is that you would be able to pray, believe, and declare the Word of God over your life and others without restraint. May it happen just like it did in the

Word of God. May it happen while and when you pray! Pray without restraint!

I hope that as you read through these powerful prayers that have been pulled from the pages of God's Word and have been prayed by men and women of faith, that it will encourage you as well and release you to believe and pray unrestrained.

May this be a year that you'll look back on and call it, "Beautiful!"

1 Abraham Prays Over Sodom

Genesis 18:20-33 (NLT)

"So the LORD told Abraham, 'I have heard a great outcry from Sodom and Gomorrah, because their sin is so flagrant.

'I am going down to see if their actions are as wicked as I have heard. If not, I want to know.'

"The other men turned and headed toward Sodom, but the LORD remained with Abraham.

"Abraham approached him and said, "Will you sweep away both the righteous and the wicked?

"Suppose you find fifty righteous people living there in the city—will you still sweep it away and not spare it for their sakes?

"Surely you wouldn't do such a thing, destroying the righteous along with the wicked. Why, you would be treating the righteous and the wicked exactly the same! Surely you wouldn't do that! Should not the Judge of all the earth do what is right?"

"And the LORD replied, "If I find fifty righteous people in Sodom, I will spare the entire city for their sake."

"Then Abraham spoke again. 'Since I have begun, let me speak further to my Lord, even though I am but dust and ashes.

"Suppose there are only forty-five righteous people rather than fifty? Will you destroy the whole city for lack of five?'

"And the LORD said, 'I will not destroy it if I find forty-five righteous people there.'

"Then Abraham pressed his request further. 'Suppose there are only forty?'

"And the LORD replied, "' will not destroy it for the sake of the forty.'

"Please don't be angry, my Lord," Abraham pleaded. 'Let me speak—suppose only thirty righteous people are found?'

"And the LORD replied, 'I will not destroy it if I find thirty.'

"Then Abraham said, 'Since I have dared to speak to the Lord, let me continue—suppose there are only twenty?'

And the LORD replied, 'Then I will not destroy it for the sake of the twenty.'

"Finally, Abraham said, 'Lord, please don't be

angry with me if I speak one more time. Suppose only ten are found there?'

"And the LORD replied, 'Then I will not destroy it for the sake of the ten.'

"When the LORD had finished his conversation with Abraham, he went on his way, and Abraham returned to his tent."

~

There is much to be learned from this prayer for us as a New Testament believer. Abraham's prayer is what we would call a prayer of intercession. Abraham is praying over a city that is filled with wickedness. God had decided to destroy the city of Sodom along with another city. Abraham is now going to God in prayer on behalf of the people of Sodom. The people of Sodom have no information about what is coming their way. Yet, the godly Abraham does. He has revelation that there is destruction headed to the city of Sodom and to the people of Sodom. What does the godly man do? He prays on behalf of the people of Sodom! He is going to God on behalf of others, that's called intercession.

That's what we do. We pray for those who need prayer; interceding on behalf of those who need prayer, whether or not they know they need it. Abraham is praying over a city filled with wickedness. That's what we must do as well. We must pray over our nation and our world. Whether they know it or not, they need the church to intercede on their behalf.

Our world is in a similar position as the people of Sodom. They don't know it, but we know what's coming. Their only hope is Jesus! They need what you and I have. We need to intercede on their behalf so that every chain is broken off of their lives. As we pray over them without restraint, every restraint may be broken off them.

Maybe, like me, you have some questions about the story in Genesis 18:20-33.

Below are some points I've pondered for a long time.

1. Why did Abraham ask God to save the city if ten (10) righteous men could be found? Why the number ten?

2. Why didn't Abraham ask God to save the city if *one* righteous man could be found?

3. If you were to pray for others, what kind of things would you pray for?

4. Do you know the people across from you and do you care where they are headed?

5. List some things which you will pray about specifically for your city.

2 Jacob's Prayer for Mercy

Genesis 32:6-12 (NLT)

"After delivering the message, the messengers returned to Jacob and reported, 'We met your brother, Esau, and he is already on his way to meet you—with an army of 400 men!'

"Jacob was terrified at the news. He divided his household, along with the flocks and herds and camels, into two groups.

"He thought, 'If Esau meets one group and attacks it, perhaps the other group can escape.'

"Then Jacob prayed, 'O God of my grandfather Abraham, and God of my father, Isaac—O LORD, you told me, 'Return to your own land and to your relatives.' And you promised me, 'I will treat you kindly.'

"I am not worthy of all the unfailing love and faithfulness you have shown to me, your servant. When I left home and crossed the Jordan River, I owned nothing except a walking stick. Now my household fills two large camps!

"O LORD, please rescue me from the hand of my brother, Esau. I am afraid that he is coming to attack me, along with my wives and children.

"But you promised me, 'I will surely treat you kindly, and I will multiply your descendants until they become as numerous as the sands along the seashore—too many to count.'"

~

Have you ever needed someone to be forgiving towards you? If you have, you have needed mercy! Like Jacob in the Bible, you read that at one time or another we all have needed or will need mercy. Why? We all make mistakes. We all do things that we may not want to do, but we do them anyway. When those decisions come back to us, we are then asking for mercy from those to whom our actions affected in a negative way.

Such was the case of Jacob, who needed mercy from his own brother Esau. Jacob manipulated Esau into giving up the most important thing in his life. Then he further tricked his own father to complete the taking of Esau's birthright or blessing. Now the trickery and manipulation are coming home to roost. Jacob is getting ready to come face-to-face with his brother. There's no avoiding it, he must face it. Jacob prays to God for mercy from his brother Esau.

We all must face the consequences of our actions

and choices. Even after a change in us, we will still face those who were negatively affected by those actions and choices. When that happens, we can ask the Lord for mercy, as Jacob did. We ask the Lord to deal with the heart of those who want to avenge justice upon us. Jacob's prayer for mercy is a heartfelt prayer.

This prayer is a prayer to pray when we need reconciliation in our families, friendships, and other relationships.

May God grant you mercy.

A few points to ponder:

1. Jacob was contrite and humble in his prayer. The Bible tells us the Lord is near to those who have this kind of heart. Is there any area of your own heart that isn't contrite and humble before the Lord?

2. Reading this prayer from Jacob tells me this is a man who no longer desires to live by deception, so he prays for God's deliverance. Is there an area that you are ready to completely turn over to God; you're done hiding and you need the Lord's mercy?

Jacob shows here that fear and the knowledge that we have the inability to provide the answer or the resources on our own, are good reasons to pray. Is there an area of your life that you need the Lord to provide for you?

3 Moses Prays to Overcome Doubt

Exodus 3:1-22 (NLT)

"One day Moses was tending the flock of his father-in-law, Jethro, the priest of Midian. He led the flock far into the wilderness and came to Sinai, the mountain of God.

"There the angel of the LORD appeared to him in a blazing fire from the middle of a bush. Moses stared in amazement. Though the bush was engulfed in flames, it didn't burn up.

'This is amazing,' Moses said to himself. 'Why isn't that bush burning up? I must go see it.'

"When the LORD saw Moses coming to take a closer look, God called to him from the middle of the bush,

'Moses! Moses!'

'Here I am!' Moses replied.

'Do not come any closer,' the LORD warned. 'Take off your sandals, for you are standing on holy ground.

I am the God of your father—the God of Abraham, the God of Isaac, and the God of Jacob.' When Moses heard this, he covered his face because he was afraid to look at God.

"Then the LORD told him, 'I have certainly seen the oppression of my people in Egypt. I have heard their cries of distress because of their harsh slave drivers. Yes, I am aware of their suffering.

'So I have come down to rescue them from the power of the Egyptians and lead them out of Egypt into their own fertile and spacious land. It is a land flowing with milk and honey—the land where the Canaanites, Hittites, Amorites, Perizzites, Hivites, and Jebusites now live.

'Look! The cry of the people of Israel has reached me, and I have seen how harshly the Egyptians abuse them.

'Now go, for I am sending you to Pharaoh. You must lead my people Israel out of Egypt.'

"But Moses protested to God, 'Who am I to appear before Pharaoh? Who am I to lead the people of Israel out of Egypt?'

"God answered, 'I will be with you. And this is your sign that I am the one who has sent you: When you have brought the people out of Egypt, you will worship God at this very mountain.'

"But Moses protested, 'If I go to the people of Israel

and tell them, 'The God of your ancestors has sent me to you,' they will ask me, 'What is his name?' Then what should I tell them?'

"God replied to Moses, 'I AM WHO I AM. Say this to the people of Israel: I AM has sent me to you.'

"God also said to Moses, 'Say this to the people of Israel: Yahweh, the God of your ancestors—the God of Abraham, the God of Isaac, and the God of Jacob—has sent me to you. This is my eternal name, my name to remember for all generations.

'Now go and call together all the elders of Israel. Tell them, 'Yahweh, the God of your ancestors—the God of Abraham, Isaac, and Jacob—has appeared to me. He told me, 'I have been watching closely, and I see how the Egyptians are treating you.

'I have promised to rescue you from your oppression in Egypt. I will lead you to a land flowing with milk and honey—the land where the Canaanites, Hittites, Amorites, Perizzites, Hivites, and Jebusites now live.'

'The elders of Israel will accept your message. Then you and the elders must go to the king of Egypt and tell him, 'The LORD, the God of the Hebrews, has met with us. So please let us take a three-day journey into the wilderness to offer sacrifices to the LORD, our God.'

'But I know that the king of Egypt will not let you go unless a mighty hand forces him.

'So I will raise my hand and strike the Egyptians, performing all kinds of miracles among them. Then at last he will let you go.

'And I will cause the Egyptians to look favorably on you. They will give you gifts when you go so you will not leave empty-handed.

'Every Israelite woman will ask for articles of silver and gold and fine clothing from her Egyptian neighbors and from the foreign women in their houses. You will dress your sons and daughters with these, stripping the Egyptians of their wealth.'"

~

This is a prayer that is a dialogue between a man of doubt and a God of promise. If you find yourself in doubt you need to have a conversation with the God of promise. In every area of your doubt, God has a promise!

God's promises bring us confidence to walk out our faith in victory. The writer of Hebrews talks about walking in Confidence.

"So do not throw away this confident trust in the Lord. Remember the great reward it brings you!" – Hebrews 10:35, New Living Translation (NLT).

Doubt desires to destroy our confidence in our walk with the Lord. When doubt comes our way, we need to remember what walking in confident trust in the Lord brings to our lives.

As you read that verse in Hebrews 10:35, you can see that confidence is something which we can keep, possess, and maintain in our daily lives, or we can toss it aside and live in fear, timidity, and anxiousness.

The writer of Hebrews is writing to a group of

people who were going through great difficulty, there was pressure being applied to them to back up off what they had believed. There was pressure to appease those applying the pressure through compromise. They were tempted to throw away their confidence in Jesus Christ. They believed in Jesus; they didn't have confidence in the walk with Him.

Do we have the confidence in whom we have believed in! Or are we believing, but fearful?

Your confidence isn't automatic, you're going to have do what the Bible says, exercise that faith. Step out on a few maybes and see that God can bring you through, He will protect you, He will never leave you, nor never forsake you.

You are going to have to decide to not throw away your confidence. What is confidence? It is full trust, belief, assurance, and boldness.

Often, we combine this word with self as in self-confidence. The problem is that we know ourselves all too well. It's hard to put full trust into someone (ourselves) when we know our own failings so well. When we know our inside hearts and lives, we know the difference between our intentions and realities. To have confidence – even the way the dictionary describes it – we need to place our confidence in Someone or Something who is fully deserving and can live up to our full trust, belief, and assurance.

Let's look at the way the Bible uses *confidence*.

It's the Greek word *parresia* meaning outspokenness, boldness, courage, frankness, openness, and freedom of action.

The root of this Greek word has to do with the spoken word and with how we speak out.

Do you have the confidence to speak out the word of God over your life and not back down when pressure is applied? Do you have the confidence to not stay on the sidelines when it's time for the walk of faith?

Are you throwing aside your confidence in what you have declared over your life according to the word of God?

Do you declare the Word, or do you hedge and compromise?

If you are in doubt or struggling to remain confident, let me give you three keys to throwing your doubt out and walking confidently in faith:

1. Enlightenment
2. Endurance
3. Enactment

Enlightenment (Illuminated – KJV)

Hebrews 10:32, NLT, states, *"Think back on those early days when you first learned about Christ. Remember how you remained faithful even though it meant terrible suffering," (emphasis added).*

Go back to when you first believed on Christ, think about how fresh your faith was in the beginning. Think about what was awakened in you when you first believed and learned of Christ. Go back to the awakening of your birth in Christ.

What is it that you want to be confident about? You have to spend time learning everything you can about it... or Him. All too often we throw confidence someone's way long before they are deserving of it. We then become disappointed. We need to learn about Christ in that learning we gain greater knowledge and understanding.

What is it that you want to accomplish? Learn all you can. Read books. Talk with experts. Network with friends who've been down that path. Enlighten your mind! The more enlightened you are about anything or anyone, the more confident you will be!

If you want to have greater knowledge about God, you're going to have to read His book and spend time with Him. I promise you this, if you read God's word and spend time with God, you will walk in boldness and confidence. There won't be any hedging of your bets.

Jesus was as crystal clear in confidence as you can imagine. They would gossip, argue, debate, and ridicule Him. His response was to walk in the room and heal, raise, and deliver. In the presence of pressure Jesus was poised because He had confidence.

Endurance

Let's look at the second part of Hebrews 10:32 (NLT): "Think back on those early days when you first learned about Christ. *Remember how you remained faithful even though it meant terrible suffering,"* (emphasis added).

The King James Version (KJV) of the Bible uses, *endured*, rather than *remained faithful*. Learning and being enlightened will only take you so far. Knowledge is great but, you also must endure. You must stick with it. This is not always easy, or fun. Look at the words here, *terrible suffering*. It was terrible, but they remained faithful. The Christian life was never designed for the faint hearted.

Yes, the Christian life leads to success, but success the way God defines it, not the common way we often think, with financial wealth, comfortable lives, and people who always love us and accept us. Living the Christian life, or keeping confidence, in any area of our lives, will require sacrifice, perseverance and endurance.

One of the reasons so many people lack confidence is because at the first sign of struggle or suffering, they give up. They quit. And quitters are rarely confident.

You will never reap if you faint.

We need bold Christians, not butterfly Christians. Nor do we need bullfrog Christians. Instead, we need *bold, confident Christians*.

A butterfly Christian is one who *flies* from place to place. They bounce, jump, skip, and hop to wherever it's easy and light. Then there are the bullfrogs. These Christians puff up and blow up anytime there is a little struggle or suffering. We have had enough of that casual Christianity. We need bold Christians who have the spirit of Joshua and Caleb that what God promised them they would possess. It may have taken longer than it should have, but they refused to murmur and complain. Instead, they remained steadfast and bold.

Enactment

"Sometimes you were exposed to public ridicule and were beaten, and sometimes you helped others who were suffering the same things. You suffered along with those who were thrown into jail, and when all you owned was taken from you, you accepted it with joy. You knew there were better things waiting for you that will last forever.

"Patient endurance is what you need now so that you will continue to do God's will. Then you will receive all that he has promised," Hebrews 10:33-32, 36, New Living Translation (NLT).

The reason that so many Christians lack confidence is that they talk about their faith but rarely move beyond talk. Christians who walk in true boldness and confidence are those who, instead of sitting around and talking about it, do it.

I once had an employee who told me all the things they could do; they could do this, and they could do that. Everything that went on, they could it better, etc.

After a few months of not seeing any results or progress on all the things that hadn't been done. I asked for a meeting with the employee, and after a good hour of hearing, *"I'm going to do, I am going to do, I can do this, and I can do that,"* in all my frustration, I just simply said, "For the love of all that is good and godly, do it! Enough with what you say you can do. Let me see you do it."

That's where Christianity must make a difference. Who cares *what* you know? You must *do* what you know. Showing my faith by my works isn't a social media post! It's actually doing what we say, and being who we are supposed to be (James 2:14-18).

You've got the talk, but do you have the walk? This may be one of the most important reasons why so many Christ followers have such an unconfident faith. They say they believe, but they do nothing about it. Their faith doesn't change the way they live.

Enactment and confidence go hand-in-hand and it's hard to distinguish which comes first. Like the chicken and the egg. The more confident I am, the more I act. The more I act, the more confident I am.

When *enlightenment* (what you know) intersects with *enactment* (what you do), and you do it with *endurance*, there will be *encouragement.*

"Such things were written in the Scriptures long ago to teach us. And the Scriptures give us hope and encouragement as we wait patiently for God's promises to be fulfilled.
"May God, who gives this patience and encouragement, help you live in complete harmony with each other, as is fitting for followers of Christ Jesus," Romans 15:4-5, NLT.

Points to Ponder

    1. How do you handle your doubts?

    2. Do you ever think that God's challenge or task for you is to expose your doubts and to trust His promise?

    3. Do you ever doubt your talents, abilities, or calling?

Have you ever asked God to strengthen you in the areas you doubt yourself?

4 Signs of the LORD's Power

Exodus 4:1-17 (NLT)

"But Moses protested again, 'What if they won't believe me or listen to me? What if they say, 'The LORD never appeared to you'?'

"Then the LORD asked him, 'What is that in your hand?'

'A shepherd's staff,' Moses replied.

'Throw it down on the ground,' the LORD told him. So Moses threw down the staff, and it turned into a snake! Moses jumped back.

"Then the LORD told him, 'Reach out and grab its tail.' So Moses reached out and grabbed it, and it turned back into a shepherd's staff in his hand.

'Perform this sign,' the LORD told him. 'Then they

will believe that the LORD, the God of their ancestors—the God of Abraham, the God of Isaac, and the God of Jacob—really has appeared to you.'

"Then the LORD said to Moses, 'Now put your hand inside your cloak.' So Moses put his hand inside his cloak, and when he took it out again, his hand was white as snow with a severe skin disease.

'Now put your hand back into your cloak,' the LORD said. So Moses put his hand back in, and when he took it out again, it was as healthy as the rest of his body.

"The LORD said to Moses, 'If they do not believe you and are not convinced by the first miraculous sign, they will be convinced by the second sign.

'And if they don't believe you or listen to you even after these two signs, then take some water from the Nile River and pour it out on the dry ground. When you do, the water from the Nile will turn to blood on the ground.'

"But Moses pleaded with the LORD, 'O Lord, I'm not very good with words. I never have been, and I'm not now, even though you have spoken to me. I get tongue-tied, and my words get tangled.'

"Then the LORD asked Moses, 'Who makes a person's mouth? Who decides whether people speak or do not speak, hear or do not hear, see or do not see? Is it not I, the LORD?

'Now go! I will be with you as you speak, and I will instruct you in what to say.'

"But Moses again pleaded, 'Lord, please! Send anyone else.'

"Then the LORD became angry with Moses. 'All

right,' he said. 'What about your brother, Aaron the Levite? I know he speaks well. And look! He is on his way to meet you now. He will be delighted to see you.

'Talk to him, and put the words in his mouth. I will be with both of you as you speak, and I will instruct you both in what to do.

'Aaron will be your spokesman to the people. He will be your mouthpiece, and you will stand in the place of God for him, telling him what to say.

And take your shepherd's staff with you and use it to perform the miraculous signs I have shown you.'"

~

In our faith journey, doubt often finds its way into our minds, hindering our belief and causing us to question our abilities and God's plans for us. The story of Moses in the book of Exodus serves as a remarkable example of how prayer can transform doubt into unwavering conviction. As we witness Moses' doubt-filled prayer to God, we learn invaluable lessons on overcoming doubt and becoming confident conquerors in Christ.

Amidst the backdrop of persecution and divine circumstances, Moses emerges as a pivotal figure. From his birth in a time of peril to his upbringing as a prince in Pharaoh's palace, and ultimately his exile as a shepherd, Moses's journey is one of drastic transitions, exposing him to doubt and uncertainty. In this wilderness setting, he encounters a burning bush, piquing his curiosity and leading to a transformative encounter with God.

Confronted with the enormity of God's divine plan, doubt grips Moses' heart. In his honest and vulnerable prayer, Moses openly questions his own abilities and hesitates to accept the immense responsibility placed upon him. He turns to God, seeking guidance, reassurance, and the strength to fulfill the divine purpose.

In response to Moses' prayer, God assures him of His presence and promises. He addresses each of Moses' concerns, providing assurance of His faithfulness and divine support. God's resounding declaration, "I will be with you," becomes the cornerstone of Moses' newfound conviction. Through this divine encounter, Moses begins to shed his doubts and embrace the calling God has placed on his life.

Moses teaches us the importance of acknowledging our doubts and fears before God. Through heartfelt and transparent prayer, we create a gateway for God's guidance, strength, and wisdom to flow into our lives.

Overcoming doubt requires surrendering to God's sovereignty. By yielding our doubts and fears to Him, we align our wills with His divine purposes, opening ourselves to His provision and mighty work in and through us.

God's promises, abundantly found in Scripture, serve as anchors for our wavering faith. We must continually remind ourselves of His faithfulness, presence, and love, empowering us to press forward despite our doubts.

Strengthening our prayer life is essential in conquering doubt. Regular communion with God nourishes our faith, deepens our trust, and instills within us a profound confidence in His ability to guide us through uncertainty.

Moses' doubt-filled prayer journey serves as a testimony to the transformative power of seeking God's presence even amidst doubt and uncertainty. As we follow in Moses' footsteps, we can conquer doubt and become confident conquerors in Christ. By acknowledging our doubts in prayer, surrendering to God's sovereign plan, embracing His promises, and cultivating a vibrant prayer life, we can rise above doubt and confidently step into God's calling. Let us remember that in Christ, we are more than conquerors, equipped by His strength and love to fulfill His divine purposes.

Points to Ponder

1. **Embrace Transparent Prayer**:
Take a moment to reflect on your own doubts and fears and bring them before God in prayer. Be vulnerable and honest with Him, expressing your apprehensions and seeking His guidance, strength, and wisdom. Allow prayer to become a transformative tool in overcoming doubt and deepening your faith.

2. **Surrender to God's Sovereignty**:
Choose to surrender your doubts and fears to God, trusting in His sovereignty over your life. Recognize that He has a purpose and a plan for you, even amidst uncertainty. Embrace the truth that He is with you every step of the way, providing the necessary strength and resources to fulfill His calling.

3. **Cultivate a Strong Prayer Life**:
Commit to cultivating a strong and consistent prayer life. Set aside regular time to commune with God, seeking His presence, and deepening your relationship with Him. Let prayer be a source of nourishment and empowerment, strengthening your faith and instilling unwavering confidence in God's ability to guide you through doubt and uncertainty.

Remember, as you embark on this journey of overcoming doubt, God's promises are accessible to you. Embrace His faithfulness, stand firm in His presence, and trust that in Christ, you are equipped to be a confident Christian.

5 When Prayer Turns to Praise

Exodus 15:1-18 (NLT)

"Then Moses and the people of Israel sang this song to the LORD: 'I will sing to the LORD, for he has triumphed gloriously; he has hurled both horse and rider into the sea.

'The LORD is my strength and my song; he has given me victory. This is my God, and I will praise him— my father's God, and I will exalt him!

'The LORD is a warrior; Yahweh is his name!

'Pharaoh's chariots and army he has hurled into the sea. The finest of Pharaoh's officers
are drowned in the Red Sea.

'The deep waters gushed over them; they sank to the bottom like a stone.

'Your right hand, O LORD, is glorious in power.

Your right hand, O LORD, smashes the enemy.

'In the greatness of your majesty, you overthrow those who rise against you. You unleash your blazing fury; it consumes them like straw.

'At the blast of your breath, the waters piled up! The surging waters stood straight like a wall; in the heart of the sea the deep waters became hard.

"The enemy boasted, 'I will chase them and catch up with them. I will plunder them
 and consume them. I will flash my sword; my powerful hand will destroy them.'

'But you blew with your breath, and the sea covered them. They sank like lead in the mighty waters.

'Who is like you among the gods, O LORD— glorious in holiness, awesome in splendor, performing great wonders?

'You raised your right hand, and the earth swallowed our enemies.

'With your unfailing love you lead the people you have redeemed. In your might, you guide them to your sacred home.

'The peoples hear and tremble; anguish grips those who live in Philistia.

'The leaders of Edom are terrified; the nobles of Moab tremble. All who live in Canaan melt away;

'terror and dread fall upon them. The power of your arm makes them lifeless as stone
 until your people pass by, O LORD, until the people you purchased pass by.

'You will bring them in and plant them on your own mountain— the place, O LORD, reserved for your own dwelling, the sanctuary, O Lord, that your hands have established.

'The LORD will reign forever and ever!"

~

Can you imagine the news broadcasts that would have been happening in Egypt during the season of the Exodus? The news would have covered the meetings between Pharaoh and Moses, reporting that an agreement had been reached only to have the decision reversed, repeatedly. Frustration would have mounted. Then the ten plagues that God demonstrated, would cause increased anticipation and frustration. If our media today were reporting, the reporting would have been over the top!

Headlines would have read like this:

"It's Midnight in Egypt but It's Daylight in Goshen!"

"Frogs, Lice, Darkness! What's Next?"

"Exterminators Needed!"

"Boil Water Order Enacted."

"The Final Blow!"

How an individual read the headlines and reacted to the story would depend on which side they were living.

Think about the two perspectives of the plagues: On the Egyptian side the plagues were meant to *melt* their hearts. On Israel's side the plagues were meant to *strengthen* their hearts.

Think about that when you are reacting to events in your own life.

Now, the people of God have made their exodus out of Egypt and are standing on the shore of the Red Sea. Egypt's army is in high pursuit and the sea is in front. There's no place of escape. Defeat or death are now staring them in the face. Moses cries out to God. The Lord then instructs Moses to part the sea by extending his rod. God comes through again and again. He provided the way of escape and then swallowed up their enemy.

Once they are on the other side, all these events are in the minds and the hearts of God's people. It is with a thankful heart that the people began to pray (talk with God) and it turns into a song of praise.

There is something which happens in our hearts when we begin to talk to God. It puts a song in our heart. Unrestrained prayer will ultimately conclude in praise. We cannot walk and talk with God and not be placed into the posture of praise. The saints of my childhood would sing the song, *"When I think of the goodness of Jesus and all that He's done for me, my soul cries out, Hallelujah!"*

That's what happens! You start talking to God, then

you start remembering the good things He has done, and you just have to say thanks. Try it!

Points to Ponder

1. Did you ever think that your praise is actually prayer?

2. Do you ever just step back and think of all the things that God has done for you?

3. Make a list below of five things for which you should offer praise to God:

_____

_____

_____

_____

_____

6 *A Prayer of Intervention*

Exodus 32:1-7, 11-14 (NLT)

"When the people saw how long it was taking Moses to come back down the mountain, they gathered around Aaron. 'Come on,' they said, 'make us some gods who can lead us. We don't know what happened to this fellow Moses, who brought us here from the land of Egypt.'

"So Aaron said, 'Take the gold rings from the ears of your wives and sons and daughters, and bring them to me.'

"All the people took the gold rings from their ears and brought them to Aaron.

"Then Aaron took the gold, melted it down, and molded it into the shape of a calf. When the people saw it, they exclaimed, 'O Israel, these are the gods who brought you out of the land of Egypt!'

"Aaron saw how excited the people were, so he built

an altar in front of the calf. Then he announced, 'Tomorrow will be a festival to the LORD!'

"The people got up early the next morning to sacrifice burnt offerings and peace offerings. After this, they celebrated with feasting and drinking, and they indulged in pagan revelry.

"The LORD told Moses, 'Quick! Go down the mountain! Your people whom you brought from the land of Egypt have corrupted themselves.'

vv. 11-14

"But Moses tried to pacify the LORD his God. 'O LORD!' he said. 'Why are you so angry with your own people whom you brought from the land of Egypt with such great power and such a strong hand?

'Why let the Egyptians say, 'Their God rescued them with the evil intention of slaughtering them in the mountains and wiping them from the face of the earth?' Turn away from your fierce anger. Change your mind about this terrible disaster you have threatened against your people!

'Remember your servants Abraham, Isaac, and Jacob. You bound yourself with an oath to them, saying, 'I will make your descendants as numerous as the stars of heaven. And I will give them all of this land that I have promised to your descendants, and they will possess it forever.'"

"So the LORD changed his mind about the terrible disaster he had threatened to bring on his people."

There are five opportune times that the devil loves to attack. One of them is after a great victory. The people of Israel had many amazing victories in their lives. However, after a great victory and accomplishment, you must remain vigilant. If you do not remain in a state of vigilance, like Peter warned in 1 Peter 5:8, you will succumb to the attack of the enemy.

You would think that through all the power demonstrated by God through the exodus and the parting of the Red Sea, the people would be well aware of the awesomeness and majesty of God. This should have eliminated any doubt that He alone was God. However, now they are at a mountain and Moses traversed the mountain for the people.

While Moses is up on the mountain, the people are providing proof positive how quickly we can forget the goodness and power of God. The small delay of Moses coming back down the mountain causes the people to begin to hatch a different plan. Instead of wanting to worship the God who had delivered them (their Creator and Deliverer), they created a golden calf and bowed and worshiped something they themselves had created.

God was ready to destroy them, yet Moses prayed for them. If the people whom you knew, loved, and led out of great bondage were in trouble, don't you think the prayer for their safety would be passionate? The Scripture declares that Moses pleaded with the Lord. That is an impassioned plea on behalf of the people.

If you look around at the condition of the people who once knew God but quickly forgot His goodness, likewise, you will begin to plead to the Lord on their behalf. John Maxwell once said in a sermon, "You don't have to be like the people who need to be saved, but you do have to like them." So many have forgotten the great and mighty acts of God in their lives and have begun to chase other gods. I pray that their eyes would be opened, yet again, to the greatness, goodness, and grace of Almighty God in their lives.

Points to Ponder

1. You don't have to agree with actions of the people for whom you are praying.

2. Is it easier to pray for God to give people what they deserve, or ask that God stay His anger and punish them?

3. Whom do you know who might need you to pray such a prayer for them? Write their name(s) below.

Make it a point every day to pray over their lives, so they will return to the Father!

7 Moses' Prayer of Repentance

Exodus 32:30-34 (NLT)

"The next day Moses said to the people, 'You have committed a terrible sin, but I will go back up to the LORD on the mountain. Perhaps I will be able to obtain forgiveness for your sin.'

"So Moses returned to the LORD and said, 'Oh, what a terrible sin these people have committed. They have made gods of gold for themselves.

'But now, if you will only forgive their sin—but if not, erase my name from the record you have written!'

"But the LORD replied to Moses, 'No, I will erase the name of everyone who has sinned against me.

'Now go, lead the people to the place I told you about. Look! My angel will lead the way before you. And when I come to call the people to account, I will certainly hold them responsible for their sins.'"

~

When Moses came down the mountain, he saw for himself the sin of the people of Israel. He tells them of the great sin they have committed. He then tells the people that he would go before the Lord to see if he can make atonement for their sin. The sin of the people as Moses described was that they were *unrestrained*. He said that Aaron did not restrain them.

Being unrestrained can be dangerous. When there are no limitations, regulations, or restraints, danger lurks. I believe I need to clarify this because you are reading a book titled *Unrestrained*. There is a difference in being unrestrained in our love for God and our faith in Him versus being unrestrained in our flesh. The Scripture is clear when we do not accept divine guidance. It's dangerous.

Some translations of Proverbs 29:18 state that the people cast off restraint.

"When people do not accept divine guidance, they run wild. But whoever obeys the law is joyful," – Proverbs 29:18, New Living Translation (NLT).

God's guidance and the conviction He brings into our lives keeps us from being self-destructive. The best way I can explain it is to look at a kite. A string attached to the kite isn't harmful, it's the only way it will fly.

Without the string there is no counter resistance.

Let's say the string is God's conviction in our lives. One of two things happens to many people: Either they don't want the string at all, so they never fly, or, once people are flying, they see the string as restrictive. Once they believe that the string is restrictive they want to get away from it at any cost, not realizing the string is what is keeping them in the position in which they find themselves.

If they cut the string, it's a crash-and-burn scene. If they try to outrun or outclimb the string, dangers lurk when the pilot of the kite no longer has control. Once the string is out of the hand of the kite flyer, the kite may fly for a while, but it will eventually fall to the ground.

If that's you and you have crashed and burned, or tried to wrestle control of your life away from the Master, then you need to ask God for forgiveness. Put the string back into the hands of the Master.

In the passages you read earlier, the pattern that Moses follows lays out a pattern for us to follow.

Moses returns to the Lord to make atonement. For us, atonement means the washing away of our sins. Here it means the covering up of sins. Moses is going before the Lord asking if their sins could be covered. In this prayer Moses gives us an important instruction when it comes to asking God for the washing away (atonement) of our sins.

Moses returned to the Lord. We should return to the Lord when we are discussing our failures, mistakes, weaknesses, and sin. Talking with other people does not bring the desired effect. We are desiring for those areas of our life to be covered, not conversation at the local diner. Go to the Lord and discuss it directly with Him.

Therefore, Jesus would say you have an advocate with the Father. Once you get to Him, be like Moses. Moses was specific and identified the sin which had been committed. We should be equally specific about our sins which we desire to be washed away. Ask the Lord to blot out, wash away, and cleanse these areas of your life.

Moses had a heart for the people that he was leading and praying for. God answered that heartfelt prayer from Moses by giving him the directive on which to lead the people.

May God give us a heart for people. Even though they are heading in the wrong direction, may we go to the Lord for them. Then may God give us clear direction in how to lead those people to where He wants them to be and then lead them there.

Points to Ponder

1. You cannot pray for forgiveness unless there is an awareness of sin.

2. Forgiveness of sin is the sole responsibility of God!

3. What are the consequences of not repenting of sins?

4. Read Psalm 86 and read the Psalm as a personal prayer to God!

Who has God given you a heart to lead?

8 Praying for God's Presence

Exodus 33:12 – 34:9 (NLT)

"One day Moses said to the LORD, 'You have been telling me, 'Take these people up to the Promised Land.' But you haven't told me whom you will send with me. You have told me, 'I know you by name, and I look favorably on you.'

'If it is true that you look favorably on me, let me know your ways so I may understand you more fully and continue to enjoy your favor. And remember that this nation is your very own people.'

"The LORD replied, 'I will personally go with you, Moses, and I will give you rest—everything will be fine for you.'

"Then Moses said, 'If you don't personally go with us, don't make us leave this place.

'How will anyone know that you look favorably on me—on me and on your people—if you don't go with us? For your presence among us sets your people and me apart from all other people on the earth.'

"The LORD replied to Moses, 'I will indeed do what you have asked, for I look favorably on you, and I know you by name.'

"Moses responded, 'Then show me your glorious presence.'

"The LORD replied, 'I will make all my goodness pass before you, and I will call out my name, Yahweh, before you. For I will show mercy to anyone I choose, and I will show compassion to anyone I choose.

'But you may not look directly at my face, for no one may see me and live.'

"The LORD continued, 'Look, stand near me on this rock.

'As my glorious presence passes by, I will hide you in the crevice of the rock and cover you with my hand until I have passed by.

'Then I will remove my hand and let you see me from behind. But my face will not be seen.' Then the LORD told Moses, 'Chisel out two stone tablets like the first ones. I will write on them the same words that were on the tablets you smashed.'"

v. 34:2-9

'Be ready in the morning to climb up Mount Sinai and present yourself to me on the top of the mountain.

'No one else may come with you. In fact, no one is to appear anywhere on the mountain. Do not even let the flocks or herds graze near the mountain.'

"So Moses chiseled out two tablets of stone like the first ones. Early in the morning he climbed Mount Sinai as the LORD had commanded him, and he carried the two stone tablets in his hands.

"Then the LORD came down in a cloud and stood there with him; and he called out his own name, Yahweh.

"The LORD passed in front of Moses, calling out, 'Yahweh! The LORD! The God of compassion and mercy! I am slow to anger and filled with unfailing love and faithfulness.

'I lavish unfailing love to a thousand generations. I forgive iniquity, rebellion, and sin.

'But I do not excuse the guilty. I lay the sins of the parents upon their children and grandchildren; the entire family is affected— even children in the third and fourth generations.'

"Moses immediately threw himself to the ground and worshiped.

"And he said, 'O Lord, if it is true that I have found favor with you, then please travel with us. Yes, this is a stubborn and rebellious people, but please forgive our iniquity and our sins. Claim us as your own special possession.'"

~

After the unfortunate incident with the Golden Calf,

Moses pitched a tent well outside of the camp. It was the tabernacle of meeting. The meeting was no longer in the middle of the people but was happening outside of them, outside of the camp, in the tabernacle of meeting tent.

Moses goes out to the tabernacle of meeting to talk with the Lord. It's here that he begins to talk with the Lord about His presence with the people. Moses told the Lord; *you said you know me by name and that I have found grace in your sight. Because of that, show me your way and consider this people and that this nation is Your people.*

The Lord's response was that His presence will go with Moses and He'd give him rest. Moses states "If your presence does not go with us..." (v. 15), Moses didn't just want the presence of God for himself, but for the whole nation.

May that be the cry of our hearts as well: *I love your presence Lord, but we as a nation must feel Your presence! Lord be with us, not just me, but with us! May we, your people, experience Your glory so strongly that we radiate Your glory to others.*

The cry of Moses needs to be our cry. *Lord, show us Your glory!* When we enter into the glory, or as we call it, "The Presence of the Lord," everything changes. Psalm 16:11 tells us about the presence of God:

"You will show me the path of life; In Your presence is fullness of joy;

"At Your right hand are pleasures forevermore."

Fullness of joy is found in the presence of God. We know that the joy of the Lord is our strength (Nehemiah

8:10). We can then understand that being in His presence is the strength of our life. We recognize that when we are in His presence there are pleasures forevermore.

Notice a very clear distinction between the pleasures of God versus the pleasure of the world. God's pleasures are forever. Satan's pleasures are for a season (Hebrews 11:25). Go for God's glory! In His presence is where you get to know Him. We should make an earnest decision to no longer know about God through others, but for ourselves.

You should know that it's far better to experience the presence of God in your life, than to hear or read about it. It is at this point in your life you will understand that a man with an experience is never at the mercy of a man with an argument.

Points to Ponder

1. Prayer is very much a matter of man coming into the presence of God. A main ingredient to Moses' prayer was that he might know God.

2. A second main ingredient was that only by God's presence could people know that Moses was approved, or that the people could be distinguished from all others. Get so much of the presence of God in your life that you are distinguished above the rest. The glory of God

produces favor on our lives.

      3. You cannot pray to God if you don't have access to God! Do you know that you have access to God? (Romans 5:2)

9 A Prayer During Discouragement

Numbers 11:1-30 (NLT)

"Soon the people began to complain about their hardship, and the LORD heard everything they said. Then the LORD's anger blazed against them, and he sent a fire to rage among them, and he destroyed some of the people in the outskirts of the camp.

"Then the people screamed to Moses for help, and when he prayed to the LORD, the fire stopped.

"After that, the area was known as Taberah (which means "the place of burning"), because fire from the LORD had burned among them there.

"Then the foreign rabble who were traveling with the Israelites began to crave the good things of Egypt. And the people of Israel also began to complain. 'Oh, for some meat!' they exclaimed.

"We remember the fish we used to eat for free in Egypt. And we had all the cucumbers, melons, leeks, onions, and garlic we wanted.

'But now our appetites are gone. All we ever see is this manna!'

"The manna looked like small coriander seeds, and it was pale yellow like gum resin.

"The people would go out and gather it from the ground. They made flour by grinding it with hand mills or pounding it in mortars. Then they boiled it in a pot and made it into flat cakes. These cakes tasted like pastries baked with olive oil.

"The manna came down on the camp with the dew during the night.

"Moses heard all the families standing in the doorways of their tents whining, and the LORD became extremely angry. Moses was also very aggravated.

"And Moses said to the LORD, 'Why are you treating me, your servant, so harshly? Have mercy on me! What did I do to deserve the burden of all these people?

'Did I give birth to them? Did I bring them into the world? Why did you tell me to carry them in my arms like a mother carries a nursing baby? How can I carry them to the land you swore to give their ancestors?

'Where am I supposed to get meat for all these people? They keep whining to me, saying, 'Give us meat to eat!'

'I can't carry all these people by myself! The load is far too heavy!

'If this is how you intend to treat me, just go ahead and kill me. Do me a favor and spare me this misery!'

"Then the LORD said to Moses, 'Gather before me seventy men who are recognized as elders and leaders of Israel. Bring them to the Tabernacle to stand there with you.

'I will come down and talk to you there. I will take some of the Spirit that is upon you, and I will put the Spirit upon them also. They will bear the burden of the people along with you, so you will not have to carry it alone.

'And say to the people, 'Purify yourselves, for tomorrow you will have meat to eat. You were whining, and the LORD heard you when you cried, 'Oh, for some meat! We were better off in Egypt!' Now the LORD will give you meat, and you will have to eat it.

'And it won't be for just a day or two, or for five or ten or even twenty.

'You will eat it for a whole month until you gag and are sick of it. For you have rejected the LORD, who is here among you, and you have whined to him, saying, 'Why did we ever leave Egypt?'

"But Moses responded to the LORD, 'There are 600,000 foot soldiers here with me, and yet you say, 'I will give them meat for a whole month!'

'Even if we butchered all our flocks and herds, would that satisfy them? Even if we caught all the fish in the sea, would that be enough?'

"Then the LORD said to Moses, 'Has my arm lost its power? Now you will see whether or not my word comes true!'

"So Moses went out and reported the LORD's words to the people. He gathered the seventy elders and stationed them around the Tabernacle.

"And the LORD came down in the cloud and spoke to Moses. Then he gave the seventy elders the same Spirit that was upon Moses. And when the Spirit rested upon them, they prophesied. But this never happened again.

"Two men, Eldad and Medad, had stayed behind in the camp. They were listed among the elders, but they had not gone out to the Tabernacle. Yet the Spirit rested upon them as well, so they prophesied there in the camp.

"A young man ran and reported to Moses, 'Eldad and Medad are prophesying in the camp!'

"Joshua son of Nun, who had been Moses' assistant since his youth, protested, 'Moses, my master, make them stop!'

"But Moses replied, 'Are you jealous for my sake? I wish that all the LORD's people were prophets and that the LORD would put his Spirit upon them all!'

"Then Moses returned to the camp with the elders of Israel."

~

Moses has been leading the people for some time now. They have been at Mt. Sinai for too long. God has commanded that they move from there. As they're traveling, they are organized and have leaders to guide them. In all of this God is showing and has shown them great care. He's leading them and feeding them.

Now as they are headed towards the promised land, they begin to mumble and complain about the things they do not have. They compare where they are against where they have been. All of this mumbling and complaining was hard on Moses. Can you imagine leading people and doing all that you can do; miracles are happening, God is divinely and miraculously directing them, you are about to enter the promised land, and they are mumbling and complaining. In all the frustration that Moses was experiencing this led to his discouragement.

What do you do when you are facing discouragement? You go to God!

When Moses went to God, he was raw, open, and vulnerable. This is exactly the way we should be when we are discouraged.

No doubt you've experienced the pain, sometimes debilitating pain, of discouragement. Like Moses, you have been encouraged, motivated, and invigorated to tackle the goals, vision, or challenges in and for your life. All this only to be surrounded by individuals who discourage you. It may be intentional by some. Although, discouragement often comes from those who have lost sight of the vision for their own lives.

Let me give a very practical tip on this topic. You need to surround yourself with people who will encourage and motivate you. The old adage says *show me your friends and I'll show you your future.* You become like the people you like, or the people who surround you. Choose wisely, those whom you allow to influence your life.

I believe that if we pray when we are discouraged, God will send encouragement often in the form of people. Keep those people in your life.

Points to Ponder

1. Can you pray for people whose negativity and threats are against you?

2. Can you have faith even if you are in the minority?

Moses' prayer was so effective, and His belief was so great in the grace and mercy of God that there was an immediate pardon, and the destruction was stopped. Can you pray with that kind of trust and confidence in God's grace and mercy?

10 A Prayer Against Rebellion

Numbers 14:10-20 (NLT)

"But the whole community began to talk about stoning Joshua and Caleb. Then the glorious presence of the LORD appeared to all the Israelites at the Tabernacle.

"And the LORD said to Moses, 'How long will these people treat me with contempt? Will they never believe me, even after all the miraculous signs I have done among them?

'I will disown them and destroy them with a plague. Then I will make you into a nation greater and mightier than they are!'

"But Moses objected. 'What will the Egyptians think when they hear about it?' he asked the LORD. 'They know full well the power you displayed in rescuing your people from Egypt.

'Now if you destroy them, the Egyptians will send a report to the inhabitants of this land, who have already heard that you live among your people. They know, LORD, that you have appeared to your people face to face and that your pillar of cloud hovers over them. They know that you go before them in the pillar of cloud by day and the pillar of fire by night.

'Now if you slaughter all these people with a single blow, the nations that have heard of your fame will say,

'The LORD was not able to bring them into the land he swore to give them, so he killed them in the wilderness.'

'Please, Lord, prove that your power is as great as you have claimed. For you said,

'The LORD is slow to anger and filled with unfailing love, forgiving every kind of sin and rebellion. But he does not excuse the guilty. He lays the sins of the parents upon their children; the entire family is affected—even children in the third and fourth generations.'

'In keeping with your magnificent, unfailing love, please pardon the sins of this people, just as you have forgiven them ever since they left Egypt.'

"Then the LORD said, 'I will pardon them as you have requested.'"

~

Here, the people are on the cusp of stepping into their destiny. They are coming to the conclusion of their exodus and entering their promised land. What a season of expectation that would've been for them. The twelve spies are being sent in and instructed to bring the reports back of what the Promised Land looks like.

The twelve spies return with good news and bad news. The good news is that the Promised Land was flowing with milk and honey. This was a far cry from the garlic, onions, and leeks that they had Egypt. This would be excellent news.

Then the bad news, there are giants living in the land. The report from the spies was that "we were like grasshoppers" to these giants (Numbers 13:33). We are incapable of conquering the land and its cities which are well fortified.

Only two out of the twelve were willing to go in and take what was promised. The ten who believed and reported the negative report won the public opinion, as well. Instead of the night being a night of preparing to possess the promise, they are rebelling against the promise of God.

So great was the reaction and rebellion to the bad news that the people were ready and willing to overthrow Moses and Aaron and stone Joshua and Caleb! What a reaction to the idea of having to overcome a few obstacles to possess their promised land. In spite of all the negativity, frustration, doubt, and fear, Moses prayed for them.

As a leader, I am sure that Moses was frustrated. One of the worst things you can do is respond to frustration with frustration. Instead of responding in kind, he prayed. What a powerful lesson; when things aren't what you desire, then pray. If others don't want to achieve their dreams and visions, don't let that affect your decision about your dream.

Certainly, in order to achieve your dream, there will be obstacles, hurdles and a few defeats. Keep moving forward and achieve what others will only dream about. That's what people who pray unrestrained do. Through prayer, faith, and God's divine guidance you will persevere and step into your destiny.

Think about the tragedy of those who were on the cusp of victory but allowed negativity to derail them. So close physically, but so far mentally and spiritually. That's why we need to pray, so that we don't rebel against our own destiny.

Go for it, unrestrained! May this be a reminder to you as George Cecil said: "On the plains of hesitation, bleach the bones of countless millions who, at the dawn of decision, sat down to wait, and waiting died." Don't die on the cusp of your destiny, go for it!

Points to Ponder

1. Can you pray for people whose negativity and threats are against you?

2. Can you have faith even if you are in the minority and the only one who believes?

Moses' prayer was so effective and His belief so great in the grace and mercy of God that there was an immediate pardon and destruction was stopped. Can you pray with that much trust and confidence in God's grace and mercy?

11 *A 40-Day Prayer*

Deuteronomy 9:18-29 (NLT)

"Then, as before, I threw myself down before the LORD for forty days and nights. I ate no bread and drank no water because of the great sin you had committed by doing what the LORD hated, provoking him to anger.

"I feared that the furious anger of the LORD, which turned him against you, would drive him to destroy you. But again he listened to me.

"The LORD was so angry with Aaron that he wanted to destroy him, too. But I prayed for Aaron, and the LORD spared him.

"I took your sin—the calf you had made—and I melted it down in the fire and ground it into fine dust. Then I threw the dust into the stream that flows down the mountain.

"You also made the LORD angry at Taberah,

Massah, and Kibroth-hattaavah.

"And at Kadesh-barnea the LORD sent you out with this command: 'Go up and take over the land I have given you.' But you rebelled against the command of the LORD your God and refused to put your trust in him or obey him.

"Yes, you have been rebelling against the LORD as long as I have known you.

"That is why I threw myself down before the LORD for forty days and nights—for the LORD said he would destroy you.

"I prayed to the LORD and said, 'O Sovereign LORD, do not destroy them. They are your own people. They are your special possession, whom you redeemed from Egypt by your mighty power and your strong hand.

'Please overlook the stubbornness and the awful sin of these people, and remember instead your servants Abraham, Isaac, and Jacob.

'If you destroy these people, the Egyptians will say, 'The Israelites died because the LORD wasn't able to bring them to the land he had promised to give them.' Or they might say, 'He destroyed them because he hated them; he deliberately took them into the wilderness to slaughter them.'

"But they are your people and your special possession, whom you brought out of Egypt by your great strength and powerful arm."

~

Moses is telling the people of Israel that he went before the Lord for forty days and forty nights. He rehearses again the great national sin that happened when they bowed in worship to the golden calf at Mt. Sinai. He was praying to God (interceding) on their behalf during this time so God would not destroy them for their sin.

In this, Moses reveals many things about his own prayer life and the effort being put into praying over and for the people. He establishes that prayer is a business that we must take seriously! If you desire a foundation that is rich and deep with the Lord then you must be serious about praying.

Can you imagine praying for forty days and forty nights for God to extend mercy? Moses had a boldness in his prayer life. The boldness displayed by Moses is not a brashness in his own abilities, rather it is rooted in something that Moses knew about God. Moses was drawing on his own experiences with God. He knew well the loving-kindness and the faithfulness of God.

Moses went to the Lord in boldness based on what he knew about God and what he knew about the people. He knew the grace of God and he knew the sin that was committed. Therefore, he got down to business in praying *for* the people *to* God.

Knowledge is power! The more you know about God the more you will understand the ability you possess to enter into His presence with boldness (Hebrews 4:16).

Paul would tell us that we can pray in the Spirit, but we can also pray with understanding.

"Well then, what shall I do? I will pray in the spirit, and I will also pray in words I understand. I will sing in the spirit, and I will also sing in words I understand." – 1 Corinthians 14:15, New Living Translation (NLT)

Points to Ponder

1. Before we will ever get serious about prayer and repenting, we must realize the seriousness of the sins that are being committed by us individually and as a nation.

2. Why do you think Moses is recounting to them the times of sin as a nation?

3. Why do you think it took such a lengthy prayer?

12 Prayer After a Defeat

Joshua 7:2-15 (NKJV)

"Now Joshua sent men from Jericho to Ai, which is beside Beth Aven, on the east side of Bethel, and spoke to them, saying, 'Go up and spy out the country.' So the men went up and spied out Ai.

"And they returned to Joshua and said to him, 'Do not let all the people go up, but let about two or three thousand men go up and attack Ai. Do not weary all the people there, for the people of Ai are few.'

"So about three thousand men went up there from the people, but they fled before the men of Ai.

"And the men of Ai struck down about thirty-six men, for they chased them from before the gate as far as Shebarim, and struck them down on the descent; therefore the hearts of the people melted and became like water.

"Then Joshua tore his clothes, and fell to the earth on his face before the ark of the LORD until evening, he and the elders of Israel; and they put dust on their heads.

"And Joshua said, 'Alas, Lord GOD, why have You brought this people over the Jordan at all—to deliver us into the hand of the Amorites, to destroy us? Oh, that we had been content, and dwelt on the other side of the Jordan!

'O Lord, what shall I say when Israel turns its back before its enemies?

'For the Canaanites and all the inhabitants of the land will hear it, and surround us, and cut off our name from the earth. Then what will You do for Your great name?'

The Sin of Achan

"So the LORD said to Joshua: 'Get up! Why do you lie thus on your face?

'Israel has sinned, and they have also transgressed My covenant which I commanded them. For they have even taken some of the accursed things, and have both stolen and deceived; and they have also put it among their own stuff.

'Therefore the children of Israel could not stand before their enemies, but turned their backs before their enemies, because they have become doomed to destruction. Neither will I be with you anymore, unless you destroy the accursed from among you.

'Get up, sanctify the people, and say, 'Sanctify yourselves for tomorrow, because thus says the LORD God of Israel: 'There is an accursed thing in your midst, O Israel; you cannot stand before your enemies until you

Unrestrained

take away the accursed thing from among you.

'In the morning therefore you shall be brought according to your tribes. And it shall be that the tribe which the LORD takes shall come according to families; and the family which the LORD takes shall come by households; and the household which the LORD takes shall come man by man.

Then it shall be that he who is taken with the accursed thing shall be burned with fire, he and all that he has, because he has transgressed the covenant of the LORD, and because he has done a disgraceful thing in Israel.'"

~

Joshua and the Israelites had just experienced one of the greatest military victories in history at Jericho. God had brought about a great victory for them. Through their obedience to His Word and the power of God working for them, the walls of Jericho were brought down. There has never been another victory quite like that.

Soon after the victory at Jericho they head to the very next battle, full of confidence. They knew that if God gave them Jericho the next battle, which was Ai, wouldn't be an issue at all. With that kind of confidence, the defeat they suffered at Ai was all the more crushing to their spirit. That crushing defeat was brought about by a man named Achan.

Through the disobedience of one man there was a crushing defeat and through Achan's disobedience the

Spirit of God was grieved. However, that wasn't the only mistake that happened before that battle at Ai.

Whether it was the confidence brought about by the amazing victory at Jericho, or a simple oversight, Joshua didn't go to the Lord in prayer prior to the battle at Ai. You could say that the events which led to the crushing defeat were like this: Achan grieved the Spirit and Joshua quenched the Spirit of God. Both were devasting to the nation of Israel.

Joshua didn't pray before the battle, now he must pray after the defeat of the battle. We should take note that prayer before the battle and receiving direction before the battle allows for praise to be offered *after* the battle. A failure to pray before will cause you to have to pray afterwards. I'd much rather walk out of the battle praising God for the victory instead of asking God how we missed the victory!

Pray. Then go!

The New Testament also gives us this same instruction. Jesus commanded the disciples to, "Go into all the world," (Matthew 28:19). However, He also instructed them to go and wait in Jerusalem until they were empowered. They needed the power of God, which would come from the upper prayer room in Jerusalem, in order to take the land for Jesus.

The same holds true for you and me. We need to be prayed up before we lace them up. Our knees must be at work before our feet go to work. You will not conquer much without the presence of God in your life.

Pray. Then go! You will either pray before and

experience victory, or pray after trying to explain the defeat.

Points to Ponder

1. Have you ever allowed over-confidence to come into your life?

2. Have you ever had an event where you failed to ask God for His direction prior to it? How did that turn out for you?

3. Why do you think Israel became so distant from God so quickly?

13 Praying for a Child

1 Samuel 1:1-20 (NKJV)

"Now there was a certain man of Ramathaim Zophim, of the mountains of Ephraim, and his name was Elkanah the son of Jeroham, the son of Elihu, the son of Tohu, the son of Zuph, an Ephraimite.

"And he had two wives: the name of one was Hannah, and the name of the other Peninnah. Peninnah had children, but Hannah had no children.

"This man went up from his city yearly to worship and sacrifice to the LORD of hosts in Shiloh. Also the two sons of Eli, Hophni and Phinehas, the priests of the LORD, were there.

"And whenever the time came for Elkanah to make an offering, he would give portions to Peninnah his wife and to all her sons and daughters.

"But to Hannah he would give a double portion, for he loved Hannah, although the LORD had closed her

Unrestrained

womb.

"And her rival also provoked her severely, to make her miserable, because the LORD had closed her womb.

"So it was, year by year, when she went up to the house of the LORD, that she provoked her; therefore she wept and did not eat.

"Then Elkanah her husband said to her, 'Hannah, why do you weep? Why do you not eat? And why is your heart grieved? Am I not better to you than ten sons?'

"So Hannah arose after they had finished eating and drinking in Shiloh. Now Eli the priest was sitting on the seat by the doorpost of the tabernacle of the LORD.

"And she was in bitterness of soul, and prayed to the LORD and wept in anguish.

"Then she made a vow and said, 'O LORD of hosts, if You will indeed look on the affliction of Your maidservant and remember me, and not forget Your maidservant, but will give Your maidservant a male child, then I will give him to the LORD all the days of his life, and no razor shall come upon his head.'

"And it happened, as she continued praying before the LORD, that Eli watched her mouth.

"Now Hannah spoke in her heart; only her lips moved, but her voice was not heard. Therefore Eli thought she was drunk.

"So Eli said to her, 'How long will you be drunk? Put your wine away from you!'

"But Hannah answered and said, 'No, my lord, I am a woman of sorrowful spirit. I have drunk neither wine nor intoxicating drink, but have poured out my soul before the LORD.

'Do not consider your maidservant a wicked woman, for out of the abundance of my complaint and grief I have spoken until now.'

"Then Eli answered and said, 'Go in peace, and the God of Israel grant your petition which you have asked of Him.'

"And she said, 'Let your maidservant find favor in your sight.' So the woman went her way and ate, and her face was no longer sad.

Samuel is Born and Dedicated

"Then they rose early in the morning and worshiped before the LORD, and returned and came to their house at Ramah. And Elkanah knew Hannah his wife, and the LORD remembered her.

"So it came to pass in the process of time that Hannah conceived and bore a son, and called his name Samuel, saying, 'Because I have asked for him from the LORD.'"

~

Believe it or not, Melissa and I can relate to so many of you who have struggled just like Hannah. The desire to be a mother and to raise a family is a God-given desire and it fulfills the command of God to be fruitful. Maybe reading about our struggle will help you in yours.

We also desire to come alongside you to help you as you walk through this struggle. You are not alone. With the help of some dear ladies in our congregation, there is a whole ministry dedicated to assist women like Hannah. *Hannah's Ministry* was birthed out of great pain. Thankfully, God has allowed that pain to be turned into a ministry that has witnessed so many miracles. We pray that we get to witness yours as well.

Melissa and I struggled for nearly six years to get pregnant with our youngest daughter. It was such a different season for us. We struggled emotionally and began to doubt things about ourselves physically, spiritually, and mentally. The battle we faced during that season was so different than anything we had ever faced. The main reason was that our first daughter came about with such ease! Melissa was on birth control and conceived our oldest daughter, so we never anticipated the struggle to grow our family. I believe that part is what made it difficult for us.

Therefore, the ensuing struggle to conceive another child was constantly compared to the ease we had in having the first child. That thought process was weaponized by the enemy of our souls. We must be in sin, there must be something wrong, those are the types of thought that would wage war in our minds. As the months and years went along the more prevalent the fight we had in every area of our lives.

Even after we were able to conceive there were times that the pregnancy was endangered. There were close calls and nights of wondering. We spent nine months on the proverbial edge of our seat.

Once she was born the enemy attacked the health of

our youngest daughter. Just four months after she was born, in what should have been a joyous time with family, instead we were praying and fighting for her. We spent that night (which happened to be Christmas Eve) in the Emergency room, battling for her health. The first few years was a constant battle. We had prayed for our daughter and we couldn't stop praying for her.

Hannah named her son Samuel, for the Lord had given him to her. She utilized the name to commemorate the struggle and the blessing. We had a really difficult time coming to a name for our youngest daughter. One day we were given the name Zoe, which means *vibrant and full of life*. It's her name, but it signifies the answer to our prayers. The enemy did all he could to snuff her out in preventing us from conceiving and then in the womb. When the Lord laid that name on our hearts, I knew that was His answer to us. She will be vibrant and full of life. We named her Zoe as a reminder of how it happened. Her middle name is Grace because it's by the *grace of God* that she is vibrant and full of life.

She doesn't realize the battle that happened, but we do, and every time we say her name, it's a reminder to the enemy that he lost, and grace once again prevailed.

Hannah gives us an example of how we should pray for our child and then keeping our word to God with our child. May the prayer of Hannah be prayed by you. May it be answered for you. Never stop praying for your child!

Points to Ponder

1. Hannah's discomfort and dissatisfaction with her life is what moved her to finally get serious with God. Is that where you are at?

2. Her prayer was so moving, so emotional, and so heartfelt that Eli felt she was drunk! Have you ever prayed over anything as deep as that?

3. How difficult do you think it was for Hannah to give up Samuel in fulfillment of her vow to God?

14 A Prayer of Praise

1 Samuel 2:1-10 (NLT)

"Then Hannah prayed: 'My heart rejoices in the LORD! The LORD has made me strong.

Now I have an answer for my enemies; I rejoice because you rescued me.

'No one is holy like the LORD! There is no one besides you; there is no Rock like our God.

'Stop acting so proud and haughty! Don't speak with such arrogance! For the LORD is a God who knows what you have done; he will judge your actions.

'The bow of the mighty is now broken, and those who stumbled are now strong.

'Those who were well fed are now starving, and those who were starving are now full. The childless woman now has seven children, and the woman with many children wastes away.

'The LORD gives both death and life; he brings

some down to the grave but raises others up.

'The LORD makes some poor and others rich; he brings some down and lifts others up.

'He lifts the poor from the dust and the needy from the garbage dump. He sets them among princes, placing them in seats of honor. For all the earth is the LORD's, and he has set the world in order.

'He will protect his faithful ones, but the wicked will disappear in darkness. No one will succeed by strength alone.

'Those who fight against the LORD will be shattered. He thunders against them from heaven; the LORD judges throughout the earth. He gives power to his king; he increases the strength of his anointed one.'"

~

Hannah had prayed and now she has received. She has received the blessing of the Lord in giving birth to her son Samuel. Samuel literally means *answered prayer*. The answered prayer (Samuel) is now two to three years old. Therefore, Hannah takes him back to the place where she prayed for him, *Shiloh*. She's heading there to worship with her family and there at Shiloh they are going to give an offering of thanksgiving.

Notice that years after the blessing, Hannah hasn't forgotten the One who blessed her. May it be said of us that we never tire of thanking God, through praise, for the blessings in our lives. We prayed for them. He answered. We received them. We should also be thankful for them.

The first time Hannah prayed in Shiloh, the prophet Eli thought she was drunk because of the heart-wrenching prayer she was praying. However, this time it was different. This time when she prays, her heart isn't broken. Instead, it is overflowing with joy and thanksgiving to God.

Hannah is there to keep her vow to God. She's there to dedicate and consecrate her son Samuel to the Lord. Her answered prayer is turned into praise to the One who answered. When she pours her heart out again to God, it's a pure praise unto Him. Hannah touches on the attributes of the God who answers.

It's been pointed out that Hannah's prayer is similar to Mary's in Luke 1:46. They are both giving praise to the God who answers. May your heart be a heart of praise to the God who answers. He still answers and we should still be overflowing in our hearts with worship and praise to the God who has and will always answer.

Points to Ponder

1. Notice that Hannah's focus in her prayer is on God and not Samuel.

2. Hannah now has a connection to those who are in need, but also to those who have had their needs met. To whom do you connect with

better?

Some suggest that Hannah's prayer becomes prophetic at the end when she speaks of giving strength to his king and exalting his anointed. If so, how did God use this woman to proclaim His Word?

15 A Kingdom Minded Prayer

2 Samuel 7:18-29 (NLT)

"Then King David went in and sat before the LORD and prayed, 'Who am I, O Sovereign LORD, and what is my family, that you have brought me this far?

'And now, Sovereign LORD, in addition to everything else, you speak of giving your servant a lasting dynasty! Do you deal with everyone this way, O Sovereign LORD?

'What more can I say to you? You know what your servant is really like, Sovereign LORD.

'Because of your promise and according to your will, you have done all these great things and have made them known to your servant.

'How great you are, O Sovereign LORD! There is no one like you. We have never even heard of another God like you!

'What other nation on earth is like your people Israel? What other nation, O God, have you redeemed from slavery to be your own people? You made a great name for yourself when you redeemed your people from Egypt. You performed awesome miracles and drove out the nations and gods that stood in their way.

'You made Israel your very own people forever, and you, O LORD, became their God.

'And now, O LORD God, I am your servant; do as you have promised concerning me and my family. Confirm it as a promise that will last forever.

'And may your name be honored forever so that everyone will say, 'The LORD of Heaven's Armies is God over Israel!' And may the house of your servant David continue before you forever.

'O LORD of Heaven's Armies, God of Israel, I have been bold enough to pray this prayer to you because you have revealed all this to your servant, saying, 'I will build a house for you—a dynasty of kings!'

'For you are God, O Sovereign LORD. Your words are truth, and you have promised these good things to your servant.

'And now, may it please you to bless the house of your servant, so that it may continue forever before you. For you have spoken, and when you grant a blessing to your servant, O Sovereign LORD, it is an eternal blessing!'"

~

The chapter in which we find this prayer I have often used as a teaching point on integrity. The conversations between Nathan and David teach us much about integrity with God and with others.

David was going to build a house for the Ark of the Covenant. At first, Nathan encouraged that decision by David. Then the Lord spoke to Nathan and revealed to him that He did not want David to build such a house. Instead, God was going to build David a house that would exceed anything he could ever imagine and that permanent blessings would come to his descendants.

David's reaction to the Word of the Lord is a lesson to be learned. Somehow, David understood the magnitude of the Word of the Lord. He is overwhelmed by the promise of God. That overwhelming feeling caused David to head in and sit before the Lord. David asks the Lord, *who am I that you would allow me to a part of this magnificent plan?* He is sitting in the presence of the Lord and the normally poetic David is rendered nearly speechless by the blessings of the Lord over and in his life.

Can you imagine being so overwhelmed by the promises of God, that you are just rendered speechless? I believe that if we really considered the magnitude of the promises of God in our lives, it would be hard to comprehend, and put into words, the blessings which have made us rich.

Ephesians states it like this: "And may you have the power to understand, as all God's people should, how wide, how long, how high, and how deep his love is. May you experience the love of Christ, though it is too great to understand fully. Then you will be made complete with all the fullness of life and power that comes from God. Now all glory to God, who is able, through his mighty power at work within us, to accomplish infinitely more than we might ask or think," – Ephesians 3:18-20, New Living Translation (NLT).

To me, that sounds as if there is really no way to fully comprehend or describe the works and promises of God in our lives. What do you do with the promises of God? You follow the example of David.

After a season of just sitting in the presence of the Lord, praise begins to erupt from the heart of David. He begins to exalt God, praise God, and to thank God. David's prayer of praise not only glorifies God but expresses stunning awe at what God was planning to do.

David receives the promised blessing graciously, then he prays *in* that promised blessing. He thanks God for it and then prays for it to be brought about in his life. When you read the Scriptures, give praise for what you're reading, then pray it in.

The old timers would say *we are going to declare and decree*. They were going to declare the Word, the blessings, and the grace of God over their lives. The Scripture is clear in that whatever we sow, that shall we also reap into our lives. When the Lord speaks over you, take those words and then declare them (out loud); sow them into your life so that you can reap what you have sown.

The Word of God (the Bible) has been declared over

you. It was written *to* you. Declare the Word over your life and pray it into your life. Every blessing and promise that's in His Word is for you to claim and declare over your life.

Points to Ponder

1. David's prayer shows he was stunned that God would make such a promise to him. Do you see yourself as qualified for the blessings of the Lord in your life?

2. Despite being amazed at God's promise, David also accepts the promise, rather than refuse it. Do you struggle to receive?

Read Acts 2:29-30. How does it relate to God's promise and David's prayer?

16 Praising for Deliverance

2 Samuel 22:1-7, 26-32, 50 (NLT)

"David sang this song to the LORD on the day the LORD rescued him from all his enemies and from Saul.

"He sang: 'The LORD is my rock, my fortress, and my savior;

'my God is my rock, in whom I find protection. He is my shield, the power that saves me, and my place of safety. He is my refuge, my savior, the one who saves me from violence.

'I called on the LORD, who is worthy of praise, and he saved me from my enemies.

'The waves of death overwhelmed me; floods of destruction swept over me.

'The grave wrapped its ropes around me; death laid a trap in my path.

'But in my distress I cried out to the LORD; yes, I cried to my God for help. He heard me from his sanctuary; my cry reached his ears.'

vv. 26-32

'To the faithful you show yourself faithful; to those with integrity you show integrity.

'To the pure you show yourself pure, but to the crooked you show yourself shrewd.

'You rescue the humble, but your eyes watch the proud and humiliate them.

'O LORD, you are my lamp. The LORD lights up my darkness.

'In your strength I can crush an army; with my God I can scale any wall.

'God's way is perfect. All the LORD's promises prove true. He is a shield for all who look to him for protection.

'For who is God except the LORD? Who but our God is a solid rock?'

v. 50

'For this, O LORD, I will praise you among the nations; I will sing praises to your name.'"

~

In this prayer, which turns into praise, are some of the last words of David. David was looking back over his life and was recounting all the occasions that God had been good to him. Look at these words which were used by David. As he is reflecting, he's reminded that God has been a rock, deliverer, shield, a refuge, and a lamp to him.

David is praising God, but he isn't just praising God for the deliverances from others but there is a praise, although subtle, for deliverance from himself.

David writes in 2 Samuel 22:21-25:

"The LORD rewarded me for doing right; he restored me because of my innocence.

"For I have kept the ways of the LORD; I have not turned from my God to follow evil.

"I have followed all his regulations; I have never abandoned his decrees.

"I am blameless before God; I have kept myself from sin.

"The LORD rewarded me for doing right. He has seen my innocence."

At first glance, you have to be shocked that David says he was innocent before God. The stories we read about David are filled with lies, adultery, and murder. Yet, David says he is innocent. The 38th and 51st chapters of Psalms are a declaration of just how guilty David was.

However, in those chapters David is confessing to the Lord. Here in the presence of his enemies, he is righteous. When, like David, I confessed to the Lord my failures, He delivers me from them, and then I can stand before my accuser, my enemy, and declare that, likewise, I am righteous and innocent because I have been forgiven.

This prayer of praise wasn't just over one event but

it's praise for the entire collection of God's provision and protection. David is providing a tremendous example of what and how we should be in our lives. His last words glorified God and edified people. This Psalm is also recorded in Psalm 18 and even the Apostle Paul (Romans 15:9) reaches back and refers to this Psalm in relationship to Jesus.

How powerful can our praise be over the great things that God has done in our lives? We must never forget to praise God for the many things He has done. Make your praise so powerful that, like David's, it is repeated for generations.

Points to Ponder

1. Why do you think this Psalm of Praise is written out twice (Psalm 18 and 2 Samuel 22)?

2. David used some amazing words to describe what God had been to him. What words would you use?

Do your words glorify God and lift others up?

17 Praying for Wisdom

1 Kings 3:3-15 (NLT)

"Solomon loved the LORD and followed all the decrees of his father, David, except that Solomon, too, offered sacrifices and burned incense at the local places of worship.

"The most important of these places of worship was at Gibeon, so the king went there and sacrificed 1,000 burnt offerings.

"That night the LORD appeared to Solomon in a dream, and God said, 'What do you want? Ask, and I will give it to you!'

"Solomon replied, 'You showed great and faithful love to your servant my father, David, because he was honest and true and faithful to you. And you have continued to show this great and faithful love to him today by giving him a son to sit on his throne.

'Now, O LORD my God, you have made me king instead of my father, David, but I am like a little child who doesn't know his way around.

'And here I am in the midst of your own chosen people, a nation so great and numerous they cannot be counted!

'Give me an understanding heart so that I can govern your people well and know the difference between right and wrong. For who by himself is able to govern this great people of yours?'

"The Lord was pleased that Solomon had asked for wisdom.

"So God replied, 'Because you have asked for wisdom in governing my people with justice and have not asked for a long life or wealth or the death of your enemies—

'I will give you what you asked for! I will give you a wise and understanding heart such as no one else has had or ever will have!

'And I will also give you what you did not ask for— riches and fame! No other king in all the world will be compared to you for the rest of your life!

'And if you follow me and obey my decrees and my commands as your father, David, did, I will give you a long life.'

"Then Solomon woke up and realized it had been a dream. He returned to Jerusalem and stood before the Ark of the Lord's Covenant, where he sacrificed burnt offerings and peace offerings. Then he invited all his officials to a great banquet."

~

In one of his first acts as king, Solomon turns to God. He headed to Gibeon to sacrifice unto the Lord. There, God asks Solomon a question.

"What do you want? Ask, and I will give it to you," (vs. 5).

Can you imagine the Lord saying this to you? *What shall I give to you?* What would be your response? For what would you ask God?

Here at our church, one of our culture points is, *Be Audacious*. In that area we often ask our staff, volunteers, and church to *Blue Sky* think. In other words, what would you ask God for, or what would you do, if there were no restrictions? What if there are no clouds in the sky? It's clear, blue, and without limit. Try that, then ask God!

Solomon asked God for a heart of understanding. He asked for the ability to discern between good and evil. This pleased the Lord! The Lord said because you have asked for this and not for riches, nor have you asked for the judgment of your enemies, nor have you asked for a long life for yourself. Because you haven't asked for self-centered requests, I will honor your request. Then I will give you the things that you haven't asked for.

There are three things we should take notice of here in this prayer:

1. *Where did God meet Solomon?* He met

him in Gibeon. The people were sacrificing in the high places, but Solomon went to Gibeon where there was a temple to God. The high places were built for worship unto false gods! God wants to meet you in the places that are consecrated to Him. Where then are you meeting God? Are you trying to meet with God in places that are consecrated or set apart for Him?

2. *When did God meet Solomon?* God met Solomon after he had been busy working for the Lord. He was then blessed to hear from the Lord at night. When we offer the sacrifice of praise or the sacrifice of service, whenever we find ourselves in the place of giving/serving to the Lord, we are in a position to hear from Him. When are you meeting with God? Is it in the hustle and bustle of your pre-determined schedule? Or are you only meeting God when the crisis has reached a fever pitch?

3. *How did God speak to Solomon?* God spoke to Solomon in a dream. Throughout both the Old and New Testaments, the Lord speaks through dreams. This doesn't mean every dream you have is significant. However, we should pray, "Lord, if You want to minister to me or give understanding to me tonight, I would love that." God doesn't just tuck you in and tune you out. Do you make time, where the world and busyness of life is turned down or off and make it a point to hear God?

Ask yourselves these questions:

- Where am I meeting God?
- When am I meeting God?
- Can I hear God speak to me?

Points to Ponder

1. Why do you think Solomon asked for understanding?

2. Does this prayer and text correlate to Ecclesiastes 1:12-18?

What would you ask God for if He was willing to give you anything?

18 A Prayer of Dedication

1 Kings 8:22-26, 54-61

"Then Solomon stood before the altar of the LORD in front of the entire community of Israel. He lifted his hands toward heaven,

"and he prayed, 'O LORD, God of Israel, there is no God like you in all of heaven above or on the earth below. You keep your covenant and show unfailing love to all who walk before you in wholehearted devotion.

'You have kept your promise to your servant David, my father. You made that promise with your own mouth, and with your own hands you have fulfilled it today.

'And now, O LORD, God of Israel, carry out the additional promise you made to your servant David, my father. For you said to him, 'If your descendants guard their behavior and faithfully follow me as you have done, one of them will always sit on the throne of Israel.'

"Now, O God of Israel, fulfill this promise to your servant David, my father."

vv.54-61

"When Solomon finished making these prayers and petitions to the LORD, he stood up in front of the altar of the LORD, where he had been kneeling with his hands raised toward heaven.

"He stood and in a loud voice blessed the entire congregation of Israel:

'Praise the LORD who has given rest to his people Israel, just as he promised. Not one word has failed of all the wonderful promises he gave through his servant Moses.

'May the LORD our God be with us as he was with our ancestors; may he never leave us or abandon us.

'May he give us the desire to do his will in everything and to obey all the commands, decrees, and regulations that he gave our ancestors.

'And may these words that I have prayed in the presence of the LORD be before him constantly, day and night, so that the LORD our God may give justice to me and to his people Israel, according to each day's needs.

'Then people all over the earth will know that the LORD alone is God and there is no other.

'And may you be completely faithful to the LORD our God. May you always obey his decrees and commands, just as you are doing today."

~

One of the major accomplishments of king Solomon was the construction and completion of the Temple. The temple was built in Jerusalem as a place that would be consecrated to worship God. The task of building the temple was enormous and costly. The temple construction involved a tremendous amount of planning and a massive amount of work and laborers.

In reading 1 Kings 6 and 7 you will find that it took thirty thousand men cutting timbers, eighty thousand cutters of stone and seventy thousand ordinary workers all working on the completion of the temple. In order to build God's house and the Kingdom of God it takes a lot of individuals pouring their talents and abilities into it.

It took seven years for the temple to be built at a modern-day cost that exceeds thirty billion dollars. At the end of the construction and at the opening of it, no wonder Solomon prayed and dedicated it to God.

This prayer of dedication is the first time we see anyone kneeling in prayer. While it is not necessary for us to always kneel in prayer physically, it *is* necessary for our hearts to be in the right posture before the Lord. More often than not, our body often reflects the posture of our hearts. Solomon's heart was humbled by the accomplishment that God had brought about by the hands of the people. Therefore, his body showed the humility of his heart.

It may be hard for us to see the similarities of our own life to this scene of Solomon's temple. However, what happened here physically is what happens to us

Unrestrained

spiritually.

In 1 Corinthians 3:16, King James Version (KJV), the Bible says, "Know ye not that ye are the temple of God, and that the Spirit of God dwelleth in you?" Do you understand the cost of the temple that *you* are? It is John 3:16 that brings about 1 Corinthians 3:16. That was the plan and the cost of your temple. Therefore, your temple should be a place that is set apart for worship! We must rededicate our lives to God. Remember, the posture of our body often reflects the posture of our heart!

Solomon's temple was famous not for its size but for its elaborate workmanship. It took hundreds of thousands of workers to make that temple into a masterpiece. For us, Ephesians 2:10 tells us that we are His *workmanship*. We are not celebrated for our size, wealth, or knowledge. We are celebrated because we are His workmanship. We should all pray that we dedicate what He has provided for us and in us to the Lord.

Points to Ponder

1. Solomon requested that God's name would dwell in the temple and that God would hear the prayers of the people. Have you prayed that way over your own life?

2. Solomon asked that God would hear and respond. What are some prayers that you desire for God to hear and respond?

God heard Solomon's prayer, but also gave instructions about how to maintain all that the temple stood for. What instructions has God given to you concerning your temple which allows you to maintain the workmanship of God in you?

19 A Prayer of Dejection

1 Kings 19:9-18

"There he came to a cave, where he spent the night.

But the LORD said to him, 'What are you doing here, Elijah?'

"Elijah replied, 'I have zealously served the LORD God Almighty. But the people of Israel have broken their covenant with you, torn down your altars, and killed every one of your prophets. I am the only one left, and now they are trying to kill me, too.'

'Go out and stand before me on the mountain,' the LORD told him. And as Elijah stood there, the LORD passed by, and a mighty windstorm hit the mountain. It was such a terrible blast that the rocks were torn loose, but the LORD was not in the wind. After the wind there was an earthquake, but the LORD was not in the earthquake.

"And after the earthquake there was a fire, but the LORD was not in the fire. And after the fire there was the sound of a gentle whisper.

"When Elijah heard it, he wrapped his face in his cloak and went out and stood at the entrance of the cave. And a voice said, 'What are you doing here, Elijah?'

"He replied again, 'I have zealously served the LORD God Almighty. But the people of Israel have broken their covenant with you, torn down your altars, and killed every one of your prophets. I am the only one left, and now they are trying to kill me, too.'

"Then the LORD told him, 'Go back the same way you came, and travel to the wilderness of Damascus. When you arrive there, anoint Hazael to be king of Aram.

'Then anoint Jehu grandson of Nimshi to be king of Israel, and anoint Elisha son of Shaphat from the town of Abel-meholah to replace you as my prophet.

'Anyone who escapes from Hazael will be killed by Jehu, and those who escape Jehu will be killed by Elisha!

'Yet I will preserve 7,000 others in Israel who have never bowed down to Baal or kissed him!'"

~

Elijah had just accomplished one of the most courageous events in the history of the Bible. He took on an entire nation, false religion, and the powerful leaders Ahab and Jezebel. There on the top of Mt. Carmel a great and mighty victory was won by the Lord through Elijah.

Now the man who had just mustered the courage to confront and called for fire is in a depressed and defeated state of mind.

This often happens to us as well. This story should tell you that you are not alone in the mountain-top experiences and the valleys that often follow. As with any biblical story they are there for our benefit. They're there to teach us to trust God and to either follow the example or learn from the lesson

The prayer that Elijah prayed is a prayer of self-pity. How often do we do that? We just had a glorious victory and great and mighty things were happening. Then a threat comes and we immediately go into self-pity.

I must say that this happens to me more than I care to admit. You would think that after years of pastoring, I would understand the spiritual war that breaks out about 3:00 in the afternoon on Sunday and continues through Monday. There's an entire leadership adage to pastors about it: *Never resign on a Monday.*

The adage is there to remind us that the fight on Monday is because of the victory on Sunday. We most often focus on the fight instead of the victory. We are just like Elijah; we forget the experience on Sunday and make a drastic, unnecessary change on Monday. We retreat to our cave and take up residence.

Elijah retreated to a cave. This shows that he was lacking confidence in God even though he'd just demonstrated the power of God. In other words, the power of God was demonstrated, but already forgotten. The threat superseded all previous actions of God and experiences of Elijah. Has this or is this happening right now in your life?

This threat from Jezebel in Elijah's life is what created the retreat to loneliness and despair. It wasn't reality it was *perception*. I understand that perception is often greater than reality. However, if you give in to the perceptions of your mind often enough it will drastically change your reality. You can begin to perceive things about people, God, and yourself that without a reality check can cause you to retreat into a cave that was never your destiny. We go into a cave and we are there alone. We often get alone at the worst times.

The Bible clearly speaks to us that two are better than one. Someone else could have said to Elijah, *have you forgotten what just happened on the mountain? May I also remind you, Elijah, you are the one who came to the cave?* As a matter of fact, God asked Elijah what he was doing in the cave. If God had sent Him there or wanted Elijah there, would he have asked the question and brought him out of the cave?

Elijah did what so many of us do: He used the behavior of others as justification of his own actions. Likewise, we must be careful that we aren't justifying ourselves utilizing other people's action or inaction.

God responds to Elijah by bringing the wind, earthquake, and fire. What a great show of power and might. I believe that what God was showing Elijah is a lesson for all of us. We depend far too much on the outwardly and the powerful to find God. In all that display of fire, wind, and earthquakes God wasn't in any of them. Instead, the power of pressing on in life is to focus on the still, small, voice of God.

I believe if you will take a moment right now, you will hear God. Shut out the distractions, emotions, and perceptions and listen, you'll hear Him! He's saying, "Come out of the Cave!"

Points to Ponder

1. Are you looking for the extreme and the flash in order to know that God is in it?

2. What circumstances happen in your life to bring the negative feelings into your life?

3. Have you trained yourself to hear the voice of the Lord over the distractions that come?

20 A Prayer Out of Distress

2 Kings 19:14-19

"After Hezekiah received the letter from the messengers and read it, he went up to the LORD's Temple and spread it out before the LORD.

"And Hezekiah prayed this prayer before the LORD: 'O LORD, God of Israel, you are enthroned between the mighty cherubim! You alone are God of all the kingdoms of the earth. You alone created the heavens and the earth.

'Bend down, O LORD, and listen! Open your eyes, O LORD, and see! Listen to Sennacherib's words of defiance against the living God.

'It is true, LORD, that the kings of Assyria have destroyed all these nations.

'And they have thrown the gods of these nations into the fire and burned them. But of course the Assyrians could destroy them! They were not gods at all—only idols of wood and stone shaped by human hands.

'Now, O LORD our God, rescue us from his power; then all the kingdoms of the earth will know that you alone, O LORD, are God.'"

~

Have you ever received distressing news? Maybe it came through a letter, email, social media message, or through an individual. However the news came, the delivered message brought with it distress.

Distress means to have severe anxiety, sorrow, or pain. The news you heard caused your heart to be troubled, your mind to begin to run, and your life was suddenly turned upside down. That's what is called distressing news.

That's the kind of news that came to Hezekiah. It was a letter which was threatening. The letter came from Sennacherib, king of Assyria, commander-in-chief of the most advanced army in the world at that time—a fighting force that had not lost a battle for one hundred and fifty years.

Not only were the Assyrians unbeatable in battle, but they were also unbelievable in brutality. They were known to put hooks in the noses of their captives, through which ropes were passed, thus joining them together in a forced death-march to Assyria. That's who wrote the letter.

Can you imagine the feelings which arose in

Hezekiah's life after reading that letter? No wonder Hezekiah was distressed! This is exactly how the enemy deals with you; it's always a threat as drastic and dastardly as it can possibly be. All to stress you out!

What did Hezekiah do? He took the distressing news and laid it before the Lord. Then Hezekiah prayed. He turned that care into a prayer. That's exactly what we must do when we receive news that causes us to be distressed.

When Hezekiah prayed, he emphasized the same thing in different ways. He speaks to God and emphasizes that God is the *only* God. This is in direct contrast to how the Assyrians believed. They believed in many, but Hezekiah knew, as you should, there is but one God.

Hezekiah's prayer was specific, and his request was that God would deliver them from the threat of the Assyrians. Hezekiah is specific in that asking for deliverance all the kingdoms of the world would know that God alone is God.

This prayer is more God-focused than focused on the letter. You will get more peace and joy by focusing on God than you ever will by focusing on the news.

May you take your cares and turn them into prayers. The severe anxiety will be overcome by overwhelming joy!

Points to Ponder

1. Do you find it helpful to spread out your problems before the Lord?

2. Why is it important to be specific in the prayers we pray?

3. Although it is not necessary to be at the church to pray, do you ever think about a place of prayer in your own life?

Someone once told me to write every problem that is distressing, troubling, and causing me pain. Write it out and then put the list away. I tried it once, I realized that I couldn't write much once I started to take what was in my mind and put it on paper. It wasn't as big a deal as I thought it was in my mind.

21 A Prayer for Healing

2 Kings 20:1-11

"About that time Hezekiah became deathly ill, and the prophet Isaiah son of Amoz went to visit him. He gave the king this message: 'This is what the LORD says: Set your affairs in order, for you are going to die. You will not recover from this illness.'

"When Hezekiah heard this, he turned his face to the wall and prayed to the LORD,

'Remember, O LORD, how I have always been faithful to you and have served you single-mindedly, always doing what pleases you.' Then he broke down and wept bitterly.

"But before Isaiah had left the middle courtyard, this message came to him from the LORD:

'Go back to Hezekiah, the leader of my people. Tell him, 'This is what the LORD, the God of your ancestor

David, says: I have heard your prayer and seen your tears. I will heal you, and three days from now you will get out of bed and go to the Temple of the LORD.

'I will add fifteen years to your life, and I will rescue you and this city from the king of Assyria. I will defend this city for my own honor and for the sake of my servant David.' "

"Then Isaiah said, 'Make an ointment from figs.' So Hezekiah's servants spread the ointment over the boil, and Hezekiah recovered!

"Meanwhile, Hezekiah had said to Isaiah, 'What sign will the LORD give to prove that he will heal me and that I will go to the Temple of the LORD three days from now?'

"Isaiah replied, 'This is the sign from the LORD to prove that he will do as he promised. Would you like the shadow on the sundial to go forward ten steps or backward ten steps?'

'The shadow always moves forward,' Hezekiah replied, 'so that would be easy. Make it go ten steps backward instead.'

"So Isaiah the prophet asked the LORD to do this, and he caused the shadow to move ten steps backward on the sundial of Ahaz!'"

~

Many times, after a season or a moment of great victory, there is another battle to be fought. Often the immediacy of the next battle sours the taste of victory we just experienced.

We must be careful that the relentless onslaught does not cause us to lose hope, nor should it distract us that the next victory is also assured to us. That is exactly the reason for the battle, it's to destroy your hope and any momentum you might receive through your victory.

Hezekiah had just been the recipient of a great victory. God had answered prayer and rescued Hezekiah and the people of Judah. God had come through and turned back the mighty army of Assyria and their plans of destruction. It was a great victory for the people of Judah and Hezekiah personally.

Roughly, in the same time period of Hezekiah's victory over the Assyrians, Hezekiah became quite sick. The Bible tells us that it was a sickness unto death. Right in the middle of victory, the battle is ignited for his health. Maybe that is you, right now. Right in the season of victory, the enemy is launching an all-out attack against you. Upon hearing the confirmation of this, Hezekiah did what I would do. He cried! He didn't want to die so he cried. However, he cried to the right person: God! God heard that prayer and added fifteen years to Hezekiah's life.

Here is something interesting: After the prayer of healing to God happened, Isaiah asked for a lump of figs to be placed upon the boil that was on Hezekiah. After that, Hezekiah recovered. The compound of crushed figs was a common medicine in that day. This tells me that God's healing comes through prayer, medicine, and through the natural healing process. In all that we can still say that it is the Lord who heals. If you need healing in your body, soul, mind, or spirit, cry out to God. He hears and He answers.

Points to Ponder

1. Is it right to ask God to change His mind?

2. Compare your response to Hezekiah's response in hearing or receiving bad news. How do you respond to negativity or negative news?

How do you respond when others receive news that can be devasting? Is your response effective?

22 A Prayer of Thankfulness

1 Chronicles 17:16-27

"Then King David went in and sat before the LORD and prayed, 'Who am I, O LORD God, and what is my family, that you have brought me this far?

'And now, O God, in addition to everything else, you speak of giving your servant a lasting dynasty! You speak as though I were someone very great, O LORD God!

'What more can I say to you about the way you have honored me? You know what your servant is really like.

'For the sake of your servant, O LORD, and according to your will, you have done all these great things and have made them known.

'O LORD, there is no one like you. We have never even heard of another God like you!

'What other nation on earth is like your people

Unrestrained

Israel? What other nation, O God, have you redeemed from slavery to be your own people? You made a great name for yourself when you redeemed your people from Egypt. You performed awesome miracles and drove out the nations that stood in their way.

'You chose Israel to be your very own people forever, and you, O LORD, became their God.

'And now, O LORD, I am your servant; do as you have promised concerning me and my family. May it be a promise that will last forever.

'And may your name be established and honored forever so that everyone will say, 'The LORD of Heaven's Armies, the God of Israel, is Israel's God!' And may the house of your servant David continue before you forever.

'O my God, I have been bold enough to pray to you because you have revealed to your servant that you will build a house for him—a dynasty of kings!

'For you are God, O LORD. And you have promised these good things to your servant.

'And now, it has pleased you to bless the house of your servant, so that it will continue forever before you. For when you grant a blessing, O LORD, it is an eternal blessing!'"

~

As parents, we try all we can to afford our children as much as possible. When we give of ourselves and then what we have done is met with less than an appreciative heart, it takes a toll. After we have given, and given, the incessant need of desiring more can be wearisome.

In the story you just read, David could have been that child who is throwing a fit about not getting all he desired. Instead of that behavior, he turns and sees all that God has provided and the beautiful life which was provided for him. When David looked back over his life and began to take account of all God had done for him it rendered David speechless.

This may not strike you as all that fantastic, except for what has just taken place in David's life prior to this prayer.

David had just been notified by God, through Nathan the prophet, that he would *not* be the one who would be building the Lord a temple. This dream was the relentless pursuit of David. He had brought the Ark of the Covenant back into Jerusalem yet he was determined to do more for God. He desired to build the Lord a place to dwell.

At first, Nathan was in agreement with David, but the Lord spoke. Nathan had to return to David's house to let him know that even though he was determined he had disappointing news. The message was, instead of David building God a house, God was going to build David a house. An earthly disappointment was overcome with a spiritual and eternal blessing.

You should try this challenge: Instead of looking at and focusing on all the things in life that you feel let down by, or wasn't enough, or feel you have missed out on, look again. In that second look see all that God has provided, has brought you through, and all that He has kept you from. Flip the script from groaning and complaining to praise and thankfulness.

I believe there is a reason this story is mentioned twice in Scripture (2 Samuel 18:7). It was worth a second look. Often the second look reminds us that God has been really, really good *to* us and *for* us.

When we take a second look at our lives, it should result in a great praise to God for the life He has given to us. Look at all those blessings and benefits that God has daily loaded us down with.

Points to Ponder

1. Praise comes from us in being thankful for all He has done. What has God done for you?

2. As you read the passage can you find the various ways in which David expressed praise to God?

Praise often takes the blessings of the past, connects it to the present promises and then extends that out to hope for the future. Can you see what God has done to get you where you are to taking you where He promised you to be?

23 A Prayer for Cheerfulness in Giving

1 Chronicles 19:10-20

"Then David praised the LORD in the presence of the whole assembly:

'O LORD, the God of our ancestor Israel, may you be praised forever and ever!

'Yours, O LORD, is the greatness, the power, the glory, the victory, and the majesty. Everything in the heavens and on earth is yours, O LORD, and this is your kingdom. We adore you as the one who is over all things.

'Wealth and honor come from you alone, for you rule over everything. Power and might are in your hand, and at your discretion people are made great and given strength.

'O our God, we thank you and praise your glorious name!

'But who am I, and who are my people, that we could give anything to you? Everything we have has come from you, and we give you only what you first gave us!

'We are here for only a moment, visitors and strangers in the land as our ancestors were before us. Our days on earth are like a passing shadow, gone so soon without a trace.

'O LORD our God, even this material we have gathered to build a Temple to honor your holy name comes from you! It all belongs to you!

'I know, my God, that you examine our hearts and rejoice when you find integrity there. You know I have done all this with good motives, and I have watched your people offer their gifts willingly and joyously.

'O LORD, the God of our ancestors Abraham, Isaac, and Israel, make your people always want to obey you. See to it that their love for you never changes.

'Give my son Solomon the wholehearted desire to obey all your commands, laws, and decrees, and to do everything necessary to build this Temple, for which I have made these preparations.'

"Then David said to the whole assembly, 'Give praise to the LORD your God!' And the entire assembly praised the LORD, the God of their ancestors, and they bowed low and knelt before the LORD and the king."

~

Have you ever heard the statement; *God loves a cheerful giver*? It is a quote from 2 Corinthians 9:7. It states, "Each one must give as he has decided in his heart, not reluctantly or under compulsion, for *God loves a cheerful giver*," English Standard Version, (ESV), emphasis added.

One of the most outstanding examples of this is near the end of King David's life. David is gathering the necessary materials and resources for the temple to be built. David begins by giving a speech about all he has provided to ensure the building of the temple. He not only gave what he had amassed through his military victories, but also of his own personal treasury. Then from the leaders of Israel to the man on main street, they gave of themselves to build the temple.

The people brought their substance willingly and cheerfully. With all this cheerful giving happening, David moves from his speech to the people to a prayer to God. What a beautiful prayer of thankfulness to God for the overwhelming generosity of the people of God. For each man, including David, had decided to give generously.

David was saying, *we have been so blessed by you God. We are thankful. We willingly and cheerfully give this to God, for all we are giving came from You anyway*. Keep that in mind for yourself in your decision about giving. All that you are giving is from God in the first place.

When it comes to giving, think about how Christ has given to you. All He has given is without restraint. Can

Unrestrained

you imagine what the church could accomplish today if the people began to give with the same measure as they have been given.

Jim Elliot, a missionary to the Auca Indians said, "He is no fool who gives what he cannot keep to gain what he cannot lose." May we all cheerfully and willfully give what we cannot keep so that we may gain what we cannot lose.

Points to Ponder

1. Do you give willfully and cheerfully or grudgingly?

2. How can you develop a cheerful heart in giving to God?

3. Below, read 1 Chronicles 29:3-5 from the New Living Translation (NLT). Are you ready to give to the Lord without restraint?

And now, because of my devotion to the Temple of my God, I am giving all of my own private treasures of gold and silver to help in the construction. This is in addition to the building materials I have already collected for his holy Temple.
I am donating more than 112 tons of gold from Ophir and 262 tons of refined silver to be used for

overlaying the walls of the buildings and for the other gold and silver work to be done by the craftsmen. Now then, who will follow my example and give offerings to the LORD today? – 1 Chronicles 29:3-5, NLT.

24 A Prayer Motivated by Fear

2 Chronicles 20:1-23

"After this, the armies of the Moabites, Ammonites, and some of the Meunites declared war on Jehoshaphat.

"Messengers came and told Jehoshaphat, 'A vast army from Edom is marching against you from beyond the Dead Sea. They are already at Hazazon-tamar.' (This was another name for En-gedi.)

"Jehoshaphat was terrified by this news and begged the LORD for guidance. He also ordered everyone in Judah to begin fasting.

"So people from all the towns of Judah came to Jerusalem to seek the LORD's help.

"Jehoshaphat stood before the community of Judah and Jerusalem in front of the new courtyard at the

Temple of the LORD.

"He prayed, 'O LORD, God of our ancestors, you alone are the God who is in heaven. You are ruler of all the kingdoms of the earth. You are powerful and mighty; no one can stand against you!

'O our God, did you not drive out those who lived in this land when your people Israel arrived? And did you not give this land forever to the descendants of your friend Abraham?

'Your people settled here and built this Temple to honor your name.

'They said, "Whenever we are faced with any calamity such as war, plague, or famine, we can come to stand in your presence before this Temple where your name is honored. We can cry out to you to save us, and you will hear us and rescue us."

'And now see what the armies of Ammon, Moab, and Mount Seir are doing. You would not let our ancestors invade those nations when Israel left Egypt, so they went around them and did not destroy them.

'Now see how they reward us! For they have come to throw us out of your land, which you gave us as an inheritance.

'O our God, won't you stop them? We are powerless against this mighty army that is about to attack us. We do not know what to do, but we are looking to you for help.'

"As all the men of Judah stood before the LORD with their little ones, wives, and children, "the Spirit of the LORD came upon one of the men standing there. His name was Jahaziel son of Zechariah, son of Benaiah, son of Jeiel, son of Mattaniah, a Levite who was a descendant of Asaph.

"He said, 'Listen, all you people of Judah and Jerusalem! Listen, King Jehoshaphat! This is what the LORD says: Do not be afraid! Don't be discouraged by this mighty army, for the battle is not yours, but God's.

'Tomorrow, march out against them. You will find them coming up through the ascent of Ziz at the end of the valley that opens into the wilderness of Jeruel.

'But you will not even need to fight. Take your positions; then stand still and watch the LORD's victory. He is with you, O people of Judah and Jerusalem. Do not be afraid or discouraged. Go out against them tomorrow, for the LORD is with you!'

"Then King Jehoshaphat bowed low with his face to the ground. And all the people of Judah and Jerusalem did the same, worshiping the LORD.

"Then the Levites from the clans of Kohath and Korah stood to praise the LORD, the God of Israel, with a very loud shout.

"Early the next morning the army of Judah went out into the wilderness of Tekoa. On the way Jehoshaphat stopped and said, 'Listen to me, all you people of Judah and Jerusalem!

'Believe in the LORD your God, and you will be able to stand firm. Believe in his prophets, and you will succeed.'

"After consulting the people, the king appointed singers to walk ahead of the army, singing to the LORD and praising him for his holy splendor. This is what they sang:

'Give thanks to the LORD; his faithful love endures forever!'

"At the very moment they began to sing and give praise, the LORD caused the armies of Ammon, Moab, and Mount Seir to start fighting among themselves.

"The armies of Moab and Ammon turned against their allies from Mount Seir and killed every one of them."

~

Fear is a motivator but it is often a terrible motivator. Fear is also an emotion that often leaves after a period of time. It is difficult to maintain the motivation that is induced by fear. In the Scripture reference, the prayer is motivated by fear of being overrun and conquered by multiple armies.

Three armies were headed for the people that Jehoshaphat ruled. Seeing the armies amassing, fear began to develop. Jehoshaphat did exactly what we are supposed to do when fear is beginning to come into our lives: he turned to the Lord. It states that he began to *look* towards the Lord. Notice that he didn't set his attention in the direction of the fear, but rather set his attention on the One who could help him conquer the fear.

Further, it states that he called a fast. Fasting is

simply letting go of the physical and focusing on the spiritual. In almost every circumstance you face which inflicts fear, it is in the physical realm. Nearly every time, the answer will be brought to you through the spiritual realm. In the situations which you face, the example of Jehoshaphat is one that you should learn and follow. Whenever fear comes pray, fast, and then get your eyes off the cause of the fear and then keep your eyes on God!

I love that when they prayed, the Scripture declares that *they gathered all their family together to stand before the Lord.* How amazing it is that when fear is overwhelming our lives, we would gather our family together and all stand before the Lord. Not cowering in fear, not knocked down, but standing firm in our faith that the Lord will come through for us.

After they prayed, the Lord declared that the battle they were facing was not their battle, it was His. God told them to stand still and He would fight for them. Often, we must resist the urge to fight battles that have to come to us, but they aren't for us. Just stay standing.

The people were standing before the Lord, now they must just stand still. Often, our first instinct in feeling fear is to take flight and run! After the answer from the Lord, had they run they would have missed the blessing that was coming their way. For after the battle was over they went and collected the spoils of the war God had brought about for them.

Stand still, saint of God and watch God defeat your enemy and then allow you to gather all that the enemy has stolen from you. When you stand in faith instead of fleeing in fear, amazing victories will be yours, in Jesus' Name!

Points to Ponder

1. When you find fear coming into your life, what has been your solution?

2. Notice that Jehoshaphat didn't just pray by himself, he invited others. Do you have friends or family who will fast and pray with you?

3. Read 2 Chronicles 20:9. Can you pray with that kind of steadfast faith?

Have you been running to fight when God said stand still?

25 *Praying for a Nation*

Ezra 9:1 – 10:4

"When these things had been done, the Jewish leaders came to me and said, 'Many of the people of Israel, and even some of the priests and Levites, have not kept themselves separate from the other peoples living in the land. They have taken up the detestable practices of the Canaanites, Hittites, Perizzites, Jebusites, Ammonites, Moabites, Egyptians, and Amorites.

'For the men of Israel have married women from these people and have taken them as wives for their sons. So the holy race has become polluted by these mixed marriages. Worse yet, the leaders and officials have led the way in this outrage.'

"When I heard this, I tore my cloak and my shirt, pulled hair from my head and beard, and sat down utterly shocked.

"Then all who trembled at the words of the God of Israel came and sat with me because of this outrage committed by the returned exiles. And I sat there utterly appalled until the time of the evening sacrifice.

"At the time of the sacrifice, I stood up from where I had sat in mourning with my clothes torn. I fell to my knees and lifted my hands to the LORD my God.

"I prayed, 'O my God, I am utterly ashamed; I blush to lift up my face to you. For our sins are piled higher than our heads, and our guilt has reached to the heavens.

'From the days of our ancestors until now, we have been steeped in sin. That is why we and our kings and our priests have been at the mercy of the pagan kings of the land. We have been killed, captured, robbed, and disgraced, just as we are today.

'But now we have been given a brief moment of grace, for the LORD our God has allowed a few of us to survive as a remnant. He has given us security in this holy place. Our God has brightened our eyes and granted us some relief from our slavery.

'For we were slaves, but in his unfailing love our God did not abandon us in our slavery. Instead, he caused the kings of Persia to treat us favorably. He revived us so we could rebuild the Temple of our God and repair its ruins. He has given us a protective wall in Judah and Jerusalem.

'And now, O our God, what can we say after all of this? For once again we have abandoned your commands!

'Your servants the prophets warned us when they

said, 'The land you are entering to possess is totally defiled by the detestable practices of the people living there. From one end to the other, the land is filled with corruption.

'Don't let your daughters marry their sons! Don't take their daughters as wives for your sons. Don't ever promote the peace and prosperity of those nations. If you follow these instructions, you will be strong and will enjoy the good things the land produces, and you will leave this prosperity to your children forever.'

"Now we are being punished because of our wickedness and our great guilt. But we have actually been punished far less than we deserve, for you, our God, have allowed some of us to survive as a remnant.

'But even so, we are again breaking your commands and intermarrying with people who do these detestable things. Won't your anger be enough to destroy us, so that even this little remnant no longer survives?

'O LORD, God of Israel, you are just. We come before you in our guilt as nothing but an escaped remnant, though in such a condition none of us can stand in your presence.'"

10:1-4

"While Ezra prayed and made this confession, weeping and lying face down on the ground in front of the Temple of God, a very large crowd of people from Israel—men, women, and children—gathered and wept bitterly with him.

"Then Shecaniah son of Jehiel, a descendant of Elam, said to Ezra, 'We have been unfaithful to our God, for we have married these pagan women of the land. But in spite of this there is hope for Israel.

'Let us now make a covenant with our God to divorce our pagan wives and to send them away with their children. We will follow the advice given by you and by the others who respect the commands of our God. Let it be done according to the Law of God.

'Get up, for it is your duty to tell us how to proceed in setting things straight. We are behind you, so be strong and take action.'"

~

In the middle of a great season of restoration and renewal of the people of Israel, there was a report (or a discovery) of a sin that was being practiced among the people. The sin was pervasive and would be a major stumbling block for the continued renewal and restoration of the people of God. As with most sin, on its face it didn't seem like that big of a deal.

No doubt the thoughts of their day are very similar to our day. When confronted with sin, the same reasoning is often used. You will hear, as Ezra probably heard, when confronting someone about a sin:

It's not that big of a deal.

Everyone is doing it or has done it.

My case will be the one exception to the rule.

I can handle it!

I'm sure you have either said it or heard those very things. However, the result predominately is exactly the same; they weren't the exception to the rule, they couldn't handle it. Nor, can you!

Why? Sin always results in destruction, defeat, death, and despair. Regardless, of the sin it will ultimately lead to a negative result. Therefore, we must do as Ezra did. Even though he hadn't necessarily participated in the sin, he is suffering for it. The sins that were pervasive were affecting and could affect the lives of all.

This is exactly where we are today as a nation. We are all suffering. Whether we are participating in the sins or not the consequences are being laid upon us *all*.

The sin of the nation is that, while some say it isn't that big of a deal, everyone is doing it. The government is approving it, sanctioning it, and defending it, therefore it's all right if I do it. There are many things that can be right legally, but wrong morally.

Although government officials, spiritual officials, and anyone else deems it okay, they aren't the ones who ultimately determine your eternity. You must live your life according to the Word of the Lord. Our allegiance stands with Christ and Him alone. Heaven and earth will pass away, but His Word will stand forever.

Notice that in his prayer, Ezra took accountability for his entire nation. Notice he doesn't say *I am ashamed of them*. On the contrary, he said *I am ashamed of ourselves*. Including himself in the equation is a powerful leadership principle. We won't get very far being accusatory.

Ezra prays an incredible prayer of repentance. It's a powerful prayer offered by a brokenhearted priest. We see neither pride nor empty promises to do better. Instead, what we see is a thankful heart for the care in which God has extended to them. Ezra is worshipful of the character of God that has been displayed to them as a nation and people. We see confession of sin and acknowledgement of undeserved mercy.

Through it all we see that Ezra displays great humility. No wonder it was a prayer recorded for eternity. It's a pattern of life and style of prayer which we would do well to rehearse.

Points to Ponder

1. What was the pervasive problem that Ezra discovered?

2. Why was this such a big deal that God would place this demand on His people? (See Exodus 34:12-16; Deuteronomy 7:3-5)

Is there an issue happening now in our society that is applicable to this story?

26 Begin with Prayer

Nehemiah 1:3-11

"They said to me, 'Things are not going well for those who returned to the province of Judah. They are in great trouble and disgrace. The wall of Jerusalem has been torn down, and the gates have been destroyed by fire.'

"When I heard this, I sat down and wept. In fact, for days I mourned, fasted, and prayed to the God of heaven.

"Then I said, 'O LORD, God of heaven, the great and awesome God who keeps his covenant of unfailing love with those who love him and obey his commands,

'listen to my prayer! Look down and see me praying night and day for your people Israel. I confess that we have sinned against you. Yes, even my own family and I have sinned!

'We have sinned terribly by not obeying the

commands, decrees, and regulations that you gave us through your servant Moses.

'Please remember what you told your servant Moses: 'If you are unfaithful to me, I will scatter you among the nations.

'But if you return to me and obey my commands and live by them, then even if you are exiled to the ends of the earth, I will bring you back to the place I have chosen for my name to be honored.'

'The people you rescued by your great power and strong hand are your servants.

'O Lord, please hear my prayer! Listen to the prayers of those of us who delight in honoring you. Please grant me success today by making the king favorable to me. Put it into his heart to be kind to me.'

"In those days I was the king's cup-bearer."

~

There are times in my life where I embarked on a project, decision, or journey and after a bit of time realized that it wasn't going the way I thought it would or should. I realized that I began the project or made the decision without first praying. I started and then after I encountered trouble, I then began to pray for the Lord to deliver me from the trouble.

I believe Jesus addressed this issue in His teachings in Luke 14:28-32 (NLT), where He states:

"But don't begin until you count the cost. For who would begin construction of a building without first calculating the cost to see if there is enough money to finish it?

Otherwise, you might complete only the foundation before running out of money, and then everyone would laugh at you.

They would say, "There's the person who started that building and couldn't afford to finish it!

"Or what king would go to war against another king without first sitting down with his counselors to discuss whether his army of 10,000 could defeat the 20,000 soldiers marching against him?

"And if he can't, he will send a delegation to discuss terms of peace while the enemy is still far away."

In the biblical account we read in Nehemiah, you will see that even though the decisions and project were certainly a worthy and no doubt godly cause, Nehemiah still began with prayer.

Prayer was not the last resort for Nehemiah, it was the beginning. This example of prayer, regardless of the worthiness or *godliness* of the decision or project, tells us prayer should be our beginning. Before we attempt anything, we should begin with prayer. Before we start our day, regardless of the agenda on our calendar, it should be started with prayer.

Over the years many have started out and then leaned on an old familiar passage of Scripture as a "bailout" for a lack of prayer. They'll quote Romans 8:28, with emphasis on *"all things work together for the good,"* implying the verse there is a futuristic prophecy of all things in our lives.

Therefore, we then feel entitled to make whatever decision we desire and believe it will work out for the good. That leads so many down a path of destruction. As R.T. Kendall would say, "If you want to look foolish in life, make your decision, and then say, 'Well God said it will work together for my good.'"

However, the wise would begin with prayer and seek the Lord prior to deciding.

Philippians 4:6-7 (NKJV) tells us:

"Be anxious for nothing, but in everything by prayer and supplication, with thanksgiving, let your requests be made known to God;

and the peace of God, which surpasses all understanding, will guard your hearts and minds through Christ Jesus."

A lot of anxiousness would be conquered if we prayed first, planned second, and then decided. Far too often we do the exact opposite. We decide, then we plan, after the plan goes awry, we pray.

You can make many plans, but the LORD's purpose will prevail, – Proverbs 19:21, NLT.

Pray that you find God's purpose and then God will give you the plan. Just ask Nehemiah, Joshua, Moses, and many others. Pray first.

Points to Ponder

1. Have you ever started out and then

realized the direction you were headed wasn't the best direction?

2. In the prayer of Nehemiah, notice how inclusive the prayer is. Do you add detail to your prayers?

3. Also take note that Nehemiah's prayer wasn't a short prayer and then off to his own will. Instead, it lasted for days. Don't stop praying until you get your answer.

27 Praying When Life Gets Overwhelming
Psalm 3:1-8

"O LORD, I have so many enemies; so many are against me.

"So many are saying, 'God will never rescue him!'

"Interlude

"But you, O LORD, are a shield around me; you are my glory, the one who holds my head high.

"I cried out to the LORD, and he answered me from his holy mountain.

"Interlude

"I lay down and slept, yet I woke up in safety, for the LORD was watching over me.

"I am not afraid of ten thousand enemies who surround me on every side.

"Arise, O LORD! Rescue me, my God! Slap all my enemies in the face! Shatter the teeth of the wicked!

"Victory comes from you, O LORD. May you bless your people.

"Interlude"

~

Psalm three is one of my all-time favorite Psalms. After reading, just like David (and myself), you may find you have faced similar circumstances which are written in this Psalm.

This Psalm is written years after David had songs sung about him. Years after the admiration and accolades of the crowds have passed David's mighty acts and wartime heroics have been diminished by time.

Now the hearts of the people are being swept away by a younger and better-looking version of David. It just so happened that the younger and better-looking version was none other than David's own son. This play for the hearts of the people to turn away from David wasn't by mistake. Instead it was a well thought out plan of mutiny.

The subtitle of the Psalm lets us know that David is now on the run. He's running due to the mutiny of his own son Absalom. I'm not sure if that is really the subplot, but I would say that it's the main plot. David is running *from* his life to try and *save* his life.

Everything seems to be turning against him. The first line of the Psalm is, "how they have increased...!", New King James Version (NKJV). When it was a small thing and just a few individuals who were against him it was easy, but now he writes they have really increased.

Unrestrained

David writes that they say there is no help for him, not even with God. What a position to find yourself in. I know there have been times I have felt that way and heard those same lies from the enemy. Maybe you have too. The enemy loves to tell you there is no help, therefore there is no hope. What then can you do if there is no help and there is no hope?

David's solution was to run, rather he's being chased out of town. When the going got tough and all seemed to be stacked against him, he ran. However, here's where I think we can all relate to David: on his way out of town and running for his life, he encounters a man named Shimei. As David's running for his life out of the city, Shimei begins to throw dirt and insults at him. It wasn't enough for David's enemies forcing him into running for his life, they still wanted to through dirt on him.

Your enemy isn't satisfied with you just giving up and running away. No, he wants total destruction. We then need to see that there is no reason to run. You'll never satisfy your enemy. If you run, that will not be enough for him. He comes only to steal, kill and destroy (John 10:10). Therefore, just keep standing there and the Lord will show up and defend you (Ephesians 6:13-14).

While you're standing there waiting, remember this: Every David has had a Shimei, Job had his comforters, Able had his Cain, Elijah had his Jezebel, and Jesus had His Judas. We all have those who rise up against us, but the Lord is your shield, your glory, and the lifter of your head. There is help and there is hope for you! David would write these words as well.

"God is our refuge and strength, always ready to help in times of trouble.
So we will not fear when earthquakes come and the mountains crumble into the sea.
Let the oceans roar and foam. Let the mountains tremble as the waters surge!
- Psalms 46:1-3, NLT

Points to Ponder

1. What is your emotional reaction when stress and pressure come? Are you fight flight or freeze?

2. Do you, or have you ever stopped in the middle of a stressful time and considered the source of the issue?

3. Selah is a musical notation that tells the musician to stop and rest. For us, it is a wise word to stop and think about what we've just read and experienced.

4. When turmoil and trials are overwhelming our lives, the best thing we can do is take a pause and rest. Read Psalm 37.

5. If we don't pray about the situations that are overwhelming our lives, we will begin to make permanent decisions based on temporary emotions. Those decisions will lead to a lifetime, and quite possibly an eternity, of regret. Pause and pray!

28 Turning Your Prayer into Praise

Psalm 8:1-9

"O LORD, our Lord, your majestic name fills the earth! Your glory is higher than the heavens.

"You have taught children and infants to tell of your strength, silencing your enemies and all who oppose you.

"When I look at the night sky and see the work of your fingers— the moon and the stars you set in place—

"what are mere mortals that you should think about them, human beings that you should care for them?

"Yet you made them only a little lower than God and crowned them with glory and honor.

"You gave them charge of everything you made, putting all things under their authority—

"the flocks and the herds and all the wild animals,

"the birds in the sky, the fish in the sea, and everything that swims the ocean currents.

"O LORD, our Lord, your majestic name fills the earth!"

~

More than likely, you've heard this adage: *The devil is in the details*. Yet, when you read the Scriptures, a different thought should come to mind.

Have you ever read the set of instructions especially through the details God gives to Moses? God instructs Moses in the building of the Tabernacle. Not only does He give Moses the minute details about the Tabernacle, but He also gives Moses, the details regarding the furniture in the Tabernacle. He even instructs Moses in the positioning of the furniture.

God gives very detailed directions in every aspect of the Tabernacle. He even gets into the details into the vesture of the priest's robes.

[You can read the entirety of the details in Exodus chapter twenty-five all the way through chapter thirty-nine.]

God instructed Moses to have priestly garments made that would be for glory and beauty. The materials which would be used to make the priestly garments would be constructed from the same materials as the Tabernacle. Why? There is always a direct link between the priests and the place of worship!

Jesus is the High Priest and there is a direct link between Jesus and His church. Hebrews chapter two tells us that Jesus would be worshiping in the midst (the middle) of the congregation, singing songs of praise to God (Psalm 22:22; Hebrews 2:11-12).

Here is a common detail often missed, especially in the season in which we are currently. There are many who state, "I love Jesus, but the church…" The enemy of our soul is whispering, and even shouting, that the church isn't worth your time, energy, effort, or attendance. My friend you will always find Jesus amidst the Church. He should see *you* there, too!

There is far too much detail for me to delve into concerning the priestly garments; the details are immense. As part of its design, the priestly garment was a shoulder piece that was joined together, creating the "curious girdle of the ephod" (Exodus 28:7-8). There was a set of instructions given, regarding stones, concerning this piece of priestly garment.

The first instruction was to take two stones of onyx and carve the names of the children of Israel's names upon them, six on each stone. Those two stones with the names of the children of Israel were to be placed on the shoulders of the priests.

Later there would be twelve stones representing each tribe of Israel. These twelve stones were each a different gemstone. The first two stones made of onyx representing the commonality of the tribes. Then the twelve unique gemstones represented the diversity of the tribes. One father, one culture, but represented by diversity. The church is our commonality, but the church should also be diverse.

Regarding the two stones bearing their names being placed upon the shoulder of the priest: The shoulder was the place of burden-bearing. Being a part of the body of Christ will require some burden-bearing, some weightlifting, and some effort to keep the body of Christ moving upwards and onward.

However, the twelve unique gemstones weren't placed over the shoulder but instead were placed over the priest's heart. Our High Priest, Jesus, carries our burdens but He also carries us on His heart. The priceless gems were placed over the heart of the priest. You are the priceless gem and you are placed and carried in the heart of Christ. All of this tells us one thing: The devil is not in the details, God is. There is so much knowledge and revelation in the details.

Upon reading the 8th Psalm we more often than not will leap right into *O Lord, our Lord*. That is verse one. However, there is information provided prior to that which is extremely meaningful. It gives to whom it was written, by whom, and what musical instrument was used.

It states, *To the chief Musician upon Gittith, A Psalm of David*.

This Psalm of David was more than likely written while he was a shepherd using an instrument that was brought out of the Philistine city of Gath, a *gittith*. The enemy's tool is now being used to give God praise. This should give us understanding, as well as giving us great excitement, about our own lives.

We sing this song of David, and it rings true still.

We were once the tool of the enemy. We were once bound up in the enemy's camp. Though, one day we were redeemed by Jesus, and now give praise to God. The enemy's old tool is now an instrument of praise to God.

That's why we can say:
O LORD, our Lord,
How excellent is Your name in all the earth,
Who have set Your glory above the heavens!

When I consider Your heavens, the work of Your fingers,
The moon and the stars, which You have ordained,

What is man that You are mindful of him,
And the son of man that You visit him?

O LORD, our Lord,
How excellent is Your name in all the earth!

- *Psalm 8:1, 3-4, 9 (NKJV)*

When we pray, we are giving praise to the Great God of all the earth. So never stop praying! Your prayer is praise to God! We should praise God that we have been brought out of the enemy's camp carried on the shoulder of Christ. Then, by the washing of the blood of Jesus over our lives, we have been made into a precious stone, carried over the heart of the Christ. Yes, He's our

Lord and we give Him great praise. I believe this why the Psalmist would command the redeemed of the Lord to say so. I am no longer a tool bound up in the enemy's camp, instead I am child of the Most High God!

Points to Ponder

1. Psalm 8:2 is quoted in Matthew 21 by Jesus. Why?

2. When you look up the heavens, do you declare His glory?

3. This Psalm shows us that God gave us dignity, destiny, and dominion. We should live worthy of what was given to us.

29 A Prayer for a Clean Heart

Psalm 19:1-14

"For the choir director: A psalm of David.

"The heavens proclaim the glory of God. The skies display his craftsmanship.

"Day after day they continue to speak; night after night they make him known.

"They speak without a sound or word; their voice is never heard.

"Yet their message has gone throughout the earth, and their words to all the world.

God has made a home in the heavens for the sun.

"It bursts forth like a radiant bridegroom after his wedding. It rejoices like a great athlete eager to run the race.

"The sun rises at one end of the heavens and follows its course to the other end.

Unrestrained

Nothing can hide from its heat.

"The instructions of the LORD are perfect, reviving the soul. The decrees of the LORD are trustworthy, making wise the simple.

"The commandments of the LORD are right, bringing joy to the heart. The commands of the LORD are clear, giving insight for living.

"Reverence for the LORD is pure, lasting forever. The laws of the LORD are true;

each one is fair.

"They are more desirable than gold, even the finest gold. They are sweeter than honey,

even honey dripping from the comb.

"They are a warning to your servant, a great reward for those who obey them.

"How can I know all the sins lurking in my heart? Cleanse me from these hidden faults.

"Keep your servant from deliberate sins! Don't let them control me. Then I will be free of guilt and innocent of great sin.

"May the words of my mouth and the meditation of my heart be pleasing to you, O LORD, my rock and my redeemer."

~

The fourteen verses you read in this Psalm are a declaration of the reality of God. David more than likely penned this declaration as he sat under the very stars and skies that the Creator created. According to this Psalm, the reality of God is found in two ways. God is revealed through His *commandments* and through His *creation*.

David begins to declare that heavens declare the glory of God. In other words, as he sat under the stars, David heard the stars' sermon about the greatness and the glory of Almighty God. For six verses David testifies that the creation declares and reveals the greatness and the majesty of the Creator.

After speaking of all the glories that nature reveals, David shifts and moves to the revelation of God not through nature but through His Word. He states in verse seven of Psalm nineteen, *the law of the Lord is perfect, converting the soul*, (NKJV).

The law is perfect. It lets us know that we are not. By reading God's Word and seeing His glory revealed, whether by nature or by His Word, there is a realization that I need to be converted away from what I am.

Look at the next three statements by David. In verse seven (NKJV) he states: *The testimony of the Lord is sure.*

Meaning God's Word is never out of date or stagnant. There are no edits, changes, or addendums.

In verse eight (NKJV) he states: *The statutes of the Lord are right... enlightening the eyes.*

When we read the Word of the Lord, He clarifies and cleans us so we can see clearly. If things are cloudy, murky, or shady then get into the Word. It will clean and clear things up for you.

In verse nine (NKJV) David writes: *The fear of the*

Lord is clean, enduring forever.

One of the articles of furniture placed in the Tabernacle was called the *brass laver*. The construction of the brass laver utilized the looking glasses brought out of Egypt by the women. When the priests would approach the laver, it revealed to them, both in its construction and its spiritual implication, their need to be cleansed. As they looked in, they realized they needed to be cleansed and then in dipping their hands into the brass they were cleansed.

This is exactly what happens to us when we read God's Word. It shows our need of being cleansed and then diving in, we are cleansed by the washing of the water of the Word (Ephesians 5:26).

David ends this Psalm with a prayer. It's a prayer we all need to pray in realizing the Creator is real, full of might, majesty and glory. It's a prayer of the need for a clean heart before God. May this be your prayer today as well.

May the words of my mouth and the meditation of my heart be pleasing to you,

O LORD, my rock and my redeemer. – Psalm 19:14, NLT

Points to Ponder

1. Have you overlooked the ability of creation to declare the works of the creator? How

often have you taken for granted the surroundings you are in and see that God is really good at creating amazing things?

    2. Compare Psalm 119 with this Psalm; regarding the Word (Law) of the Lord.

How often have asked God to provide, protect, or to please your desire, without being obedient to His Word?

30 The 23rd Psalm

Psalm 23:1-6

A psalm of David.

"The LORD is my shepherd; I have all that I need.

"He lets me rest in green meadows; he leads me beside peaceful streams.

"He renews my strength. He guides me along right paths, bringing honor to his name.

"Even when I walk through the darkest valley, I will not be afraid, for you are close beside me. Your rod and your staff protect and comfort me.

"You prepare a feast for me in the presence of my enemies. You honor me by anointing my head with oil. My cup overflows with blessings.

"Surely your goodness and unfailing love will pursue me all the days of my life, "and I will live in the house of the LORD forever."

~

No doubt you've either read or heard the 23rd Psalm. This powerful and popular Psalm is read on many occasions. Although it is also used as a memorial at funerals, it is a Psalm of comfort and promise. It is a *Psalm of Victory*.

There is much discussion as to when David wrote it. Some say, according to verse four, David wrote in the later years of his life. Others read verse five and say it was written during the rebellion of his son Absalom. Some even say he wrote it when he was a young shepherd watching and tending to his father's herds on the hills and wilderness of Israel. Regardless, these six verses speak to us and offer us hope and faith in every circumstance we may face.

It could be that you will read it in the midst of trial, turmoil, and trouble. Or you could be reading it right after a great and spiritual victory which has caused you to be misunderstood and created enemies you never had before. You could even be reading it and find yourself in the middle of others trying to rob and steal what is rightfully yours. Regardless the six verses will create hope in the middle of your despair. It will bring hope and comfort as you traverse the lonely valleys of victory. It will stir faith in you when you see that you will overcome just as did David.

As you read the Psalm you automatically see this is

a *you-and-Him-relationship*. No one else matters when it comes down to it. It's about you and your walk with the Lord. Victory belongs to God and if you are with Him, then you will have victory. The lonely path of the valley is ultimately a pathway to a great banquet served by the King of kings. Don't allow the threats of the valley to deter you from the mountaintop experiences.

One note though is that David learned many lessons while in the wilderness, valleys, and shepherding which served him well as king. Likewise, there are many lessons you have learned along the path to where your destiny lay. Those lessons will serve you well.

David was taken from the wilderness to the Palace. From the folds of sheep to the presses of crowds. He was taken from lions and bears to giants on the battlefield. He went from shepherd to king, but the same lessons applied. In order to be successful and overcoming, whether it was a lion or Goliath, keeping sheep or governing the kingdom, valleys or mountains, David needed the Lord. That lesson is one we would do well to learn and practice every day.

Points to Ponder

1. One of the boldest statements in the Psalm is, "I will fear no evil." Can you say that? How can you come to a place in your walk with the Shepherd in which you will not fear?

2. Look at how wonderfully the shepherd takes care of His sheep.

3. We all walk the valley described here. How can you walk it in faith?

31 A Prayer of Forgiveness

Psalm 51:1-19

"For the choir director: A psalm of David, regarding the time Nathan the prophet came to him after David had committed adultery with Bathsheba.

"Have mercy on me, O God, because of your unfailing love. Because of your great compassion, blot out the stain of my sins.

"Wash me clean from my guilt. Purify me from my sin.

"For I recognize my rebellion; it haunts me day and night.

"Against you, and you alone, have I sinned; I have done what is evil in your sight. You will be proved right in what you say, and your judgment against me is just.

"For I was born a sinner— yes, from the moment my mother conceived me.

"But you desire honesty from the womb, teaching me wisdom even there.

"Purify me from my sins, and I will be clean; wash me, and I will be whiter than snow.

"Oh, give me back my joy again; you have broken me— now let me rejoice.

"Don't keep looking at my sins. Remove the stain of my guilt.

"Create in me a clean heart, O God. Renew a loyal spirit within me.

"Do not banish me from your presence, and don't take your Holy Spirit from me.

"Restore to me the joy of your salvation, and make me willing to obey you.

"Then I will teach your ways to rebels, and they will return to you.

"Forgive me for shedding blood, O God who saves; then I will joyfully sing of your forgiveness.

"Unseal my lips, O Lord, that my mouth may praise you.

"You do not desire a sacrifice, or I would offer one. You do not want a burnt offering.

"The sacrifice you desire is a broken spirit. You will not reject a broken and repentant heart, O God.

"Look with favor on Zion and help her; rebuild the walls of Jerusalem.

"Then you will be pleased with sacrifices offered in the right spirit— with burnt offerings and whole burnt offerings. Then bulls will again be sacrificed on your altar."

Psalm 139:23-24

"Search me, O God, and know my heart; test me and know my anxious thoughts.

"Point out anything in me that offends you and lead me along the path of everlasting life."

~

The same guy wrote Psalm 139:23-24 where he asks with boldness that the Lord would search him test him and know his anxious thoughts… point out anything that offends you. A Psalm written in boldness and confidence in God. This is the same guy who wrote Psalm 51 who wasn't willing to bear his heart until he'd been confronted by the prophet Nathan.

The confrontation with Nathan was over the sin committed in regard to a woman named Bathsheba. After a massive attempt to cover up the sin, God sends Nathan to bring David to a place of repentance. Psalm 51 is a response to that confrontation.

Conviction, which is brought to us by any means, is the proper response to God. The response wasn't offense but brokenness.

David wrote Psalm 139 with boldness. He wrote Psalm 51 with brokenness. He wrote Psalm 23 plucking the strings of his harp. He wrote psalm 51 plucking the strings of his heart. He doesn't blame anybody for his sin. He makes no allusion to Bathsheba. Instead, David is painfully personal. He asks to be purified, to be made clean. He asks to be washed and made white as snow.

There is a request for restoration and renewing of the right things. Seeing that should speak to us what sin does. Sin destroys, steals, and kills. However, grace and mercy are here to renew, restore and revive.

We get the restoration, renewal, and the reviving by turning to God in repentance. It is through repentance we go from brokenness to boldness.

Points to Ponder

1. David utilizes four different words for his violation of God's will for his life.
- *Transgressions*: Depicts a spirit of defiant disobedience against God.
- *Iniquity*: Represents a perversion, a distortion of that which is true or good versus that which is altogether wrong.
- *Sin*: Denotes a missing of the mark, a deficiency with respect to intent or purpose.
- *Evil*: That which is actually wrong.

2. The word "create" in Psalm 51:10 is the same word in Genesis 1:1. It is suggested that in both places God creates something out of nothing. In Psalm 51, what David is asking for is a new heart, not a renovated, rebuilt old one.

3. Have you asked God to forgive you?

Have you developed a broken and contrite heart with God so you can move from brokenness to boldness?

32 A Prayer for Guidance and Understanding

Psalm 139:1-24

"O LORD, you have examined my heart and know everything about me.

"You know when I sit down or stand up. You know my thoughts even when I'm far away.

"You see me when I travel and when I rest at home. You know everything I do.

"You know what I am going to say even before I say it, LORD.

"You go before me and follow me. You place your hand of blessing on my head.

"Such knowledge is too wonderful for me, too great for me to understand!

"I can never escape from your Spirit! I can never get away from your presence!

"If I go up to heaven, you are there; if I go down to

the grave, you are there.

"If I ride the wings of the morning, if I dwell by the farthest oceans,

"even there your hand will guide me, and your strength will support me.

"I could ask the darkness to hide me and the light around me to become night—

"but even in darkness I cannot hide from you. To you the night shines as bright as day.

Darkness and light are the same to you.

"You made all the delicate, inner parts of my body and knit me together in my mother's womb.

"Thank you for making me so wonderfully complex! Your workmanship is marvelous—how well I know it.

"You watched me as I was being formed in utter seclusion, as I was woven together in the dark of the womb.

"You saw me before I was born. Every day of my life was recorded in your book.

"Every moment was laid out before a single day had passed.

"How precious are your thoughts about me, O God. They cannot be numbered!

"I can't even count them; they outnumber the grains of sand! And when I wake up,

you are still with me!

"O God, if only you would destroy the wicked! Get out of my life, you murderers!

"They blaspheme you; your enemies misuse your

name.

"O LORD, shouldn't I hate those who hate you? Shouldn't I despise those who oppose you?

"Yes, I hate them with total hatred, for your enemies are my enemies.

"Search me, O God, and know my heart; test me and know my anxious thoughts.

"Point out anything in me that offends you, and lead me along the path of everlasting life."

~

As David writes this powerful Psalm, he opens by saying, *Lord, you know me! You know when I am having a good day and when I am having a bad day.* The Lord knows you that well too.

Then David says, *You know every word that is on my tongue.* Every word that you speak is heard in heaven. Jesus said in Matthew 12:37 (NKJV), "For by your words you will be justified, and by your words you will be condemned." That should change the way you speak about others and about yourself. Every word is broadcast into the heavens.

The power of your words is an important lesson to learn. Many speak terribly about themselves, degrading and deprecating the handiwork of God. You say I'm talking about myself; it surely doesn't matter? It does!

Read what David wrote in Psalm 139:13-16, New King James Version (NKJV):

Unrestrained

> *For You formed my inward parts; You covered me in my mother's womb.*
>
> *I will praise You, for I am fearfully and wonderfully made; Marvelous are Your works, And that my soul knows very well.*
>
> *My frame was not hidden from You, When I was made in secret, And skillfully wrought in the lowest parts of the earth.*
>
> *Your eyes saw my substance, being yet unformed. And in Your book they all were written, The days fashioned for me, When as yet there were none of them.*

In other words, God put us together exactly the way He desired us to be. Therefore, when we criticize and degrade ourselves, we are degrading the work of God and then God Himself. We begin to question God. Why did You make me this way? Why don't I have this talent or this ability? Why was a born with this uniqueness?

Could it be that God gave you the talents and the abilities which you have *on purpose?* God certainly has a purpose for you. We must begin to ask God for guidance and understanding in who we are, what we were purposed for, and then walk out that purpose.

This reminds me of a man in the Bible named Ehud. Never heard of him? He was born into the tribe of Benjamin. Benjamin means *the son of my right hand.* However, Ehud was born *left-handed.* Ehud may have thought; God has made a mistake in making and forming me. I am supposed to be right-handed and here I am left-handed.

I know for myself growing up left-handed offered some unique challenges and in playing sports, some teasing of how I was backwards and other teasing. Here, Ehud is in a tribe called the *Right Handers* and he's left-handed. There may have been some who questioned his worth, abilities, and his confidence lacking.

Until one day when he was asked to carry out an assignment: to assassinate Eglon, the wicked king of Moab. Ehud hid a two-edged dagger underneath his cloak and strapped it to his right side so that he could draw it across his body with his left hand. When he went into the presence of Eglon, the king's bodyguards assumed that he, a Benjamite was right-handed and only frisked his left side. Maybe it was at that moment in which Ehud understood why he was left-handed. He completed his mission and Israel was free of Eglon's wicked rule because the Lord knew what He was doing all along (Judges 3).

As He did with Ehud, the Lord has designed *you* for a specific purpose. You might not know what it is for years but at a certain point, if you're observant, you'll begin to see why you are the way you are. Your duty is to ask God for understanding and guidance along the way and be ready for your Ehud moment.

Points to Ponder

1. How does God knowing you so well,

impact the decisions that you make?

2. Do you ever feel the sense of purpose and destiny that, *I was born for this moment*?

Are you prepared for the Ehud assignment in your life?

33 A Prayer for His Presence

Isaiah 64:1-9

"Oh, that you would burst from the heavens and come down! How the mountains would quake in your presence!

"As fire causes wood to burn and water to boil, your coming would make the nations tremble. Then your enemies would learn the reason for your fame!

"When you came down long ago, you did awesome deeds beyond our highest expectations. And oh, how the mountains quaked!

"For since the world began, no ear has heard and no eye has seen a God like you, who works for those who wait for him!

"You welcome those who gladly do good, who follow godly ways. But you have been very angry with us, for we are not godly. We are constant sinners; how can people like us be saved?

"We are all infected and impure with sin. When we display our righteous deeds, they are nothing but filthy rags. Like autumn leaves, we wither and fall, and our sins sweep us away like the wind.

"Yet no one calls on your name or pleads with you for mercy. Therefore, you have turned away from us and turned us over to our sins.

"And yet, O LORD, you are our Father. We are the clay, and you are the potter. We all are formed by your hand.

"Don't be so angry with us, LORD. Please don't remember our sins forever. Look at us, we pray, and see that we are all your people."

~

Isaiah, the Psalmist David of Psalm 37, and the Apostle Paul all state much of what my heart desires and what I pray for. May it be your desire as well. I just want to be in the presence of God!

Paul said in 1 Corinthians 2:9 (KJV), "But as it is written, Eye hath not seen, nor ear heard, neither have entered into the heart of man, the things which God hath prepared for them that love him."

In all that we have witnessed, seen, heard, felt, touched, and experienced, none of that compares to what God can do, will do, and desires to do. That is pretty incredible to think about. Take all you have experienced and lay that down next to what God can do. It's not even close.

This is what Isaiah stated:

Oh, that you would burst from the heavens and come down! How the mountains would quake in your presence!

As fire causes wood to burn and water to boil, your coming would make the nations tremble. Then your enemies would learn the reason for your fame!

When you came down long ago, you did awesome deeds beyond our highest expectations. And oh, how the mountains quaked!

For since the world began, no ear has heard and no eye has seen a God like you,

who works for those who wait for him! – Isaiah 64:1-4, NLT.

May our prayer be that God would burst from the heavens and come down. Then people of the world would know why this God of ours has the fame that He has. He will do works and wonders that are beyond our highest expectations.

What are your highest expectations? Do you realize that expectancy is the birthplace of the miraculous? James said, "you have not because you ask not," James 4:2, King James Version (KJV). You will never ask if you don't have the expectation that it is possible to receive what you are asking for. Jesus said, "Ask and it will be given…"

In Psalm 37:4 (NLT), David said, "Take delight in

the LORD, and he will give you your heart's desires."

What is the desire of your heart? True and right desires come from delighting in the presence of the Lord. When God bursts forth and comes down, you will delight in His presence. Your heart will have a desire, then out of the abundance of the heart the mouth will speak, or shall I say ask, and it will be given!

Our prayer should then be, *may Your presence fill this place*. May we have His presence and then in His presence there are presents.

Points to Ponder

1. Have you ever thought about what it would be like to walk with Jesus after witnessing one of the miracles?

2. If you were hungry and had witnessed or heard about the feeding of the five thousand, what would you ask Jesus for?

3. Do you know how to *delight* in the presence of the Lord?

Further study: Ephesians 3:20; Psalm 16:11; James 4:2; Matthew 7:7

34 *A Prayer for Clarification*

Jeremiah 32:16-27

Jeremiah's Prayer
"Then after I had given the papers to Baruch, I prayed to the LORD:

'O Sovereign LORD! You made the heavens and earth by your strong hand and powerful arm. Nothing is too hard for you!

'You show unfailing love to thousands, but you also bring the consequences of one generation's sin upon the next. You are the great and powerful God, the LORD of Heaven's Armies.

'You have all wisdom and do great and mighty miracles. You see the conduct of all people, and you give them what they deserve.

'You performed miraculous signs and wonders in the land of Egypt—things still remembered to this day!

Unrestrained

And you have continued to do great miracles in Israel and all around the world. You have made your name famous to this day.

'You brought Israel out of Egypt with mighty signs and wonders, with a strong hand and powerful arm, and with overwhelming terror.

'You gave the people of Israel this land that you had promised their ancestors long before—a land flowing with milk and honey.

'Our ancestors came and conquered it and lived in it, but they refused to obey you or follow your word. They have not done anything you commanded. That is why you have sent this terrible disaster upon them.

'See how the siege ramps have been built against the city walls! Through war, famine, and disease, the city will be handed over to the Babylonians, who will conquer it. Everything has happened just as you said.

'And yet, O Sovereign LORD, you have told me to buy the field—paying good money for it before these witnesses—even though the city will soon be handed over to the Babylonians.'

"Then this message came to Jeremiah from the LORD:

'I am the LORD, the God of all the peoples of the world. Is anything too hard for me?'"

~

Jeremiah is praying a prayer to God after much

confusion and then confirmation of the Word of the Lord. Jeremiah is still needing confirmation from God! A better way to say it is that Jeremiah is need of divine direction. Everything around him is saying one thing yet he hears God saying something that goes against what he is seeing.

Certainly, our day is a day of confusion. Everything we hear, see, and experience testifies to confusion. We, like Jeremiah, need to hear directly from God for our direction. Even then, the direction we often receive from God can confuse, because it often runs contrary to everything that is going on around us. This is why we must pray. The only way to have clear direction is to pray and listen to the voice of God.

We should take heart. Even Jeremiah needed clarification and confirmation. What did he do? He prayed.

He prayed unto the Lord. He stated exactly what he knew about God and how God had acted and performed in the past, believing that God would once again perform as He had previously.

In verse 17 Jeremiah said, "There's nothing too hard for you, Lord." He's saying that, calming his own anxiety about the situation. Then ten verses later, God responds using the same words as Jeremiah: "Is there anything too hard for me?"

The Lord is repeating back to Jeremiah the very prayer he prayed. I have found that is the beauty of prayer. We will often find ourselves declaring the very answer we need. Oftentimes, we get the solution to our situation simply in the prayer we prayed. We gain direction, clarification, and guidance through the very act of praying. Here the Lord gave Jeremiah the answer to his prayer by repeating his own prayer back to him. Is anything too hard for the Lord?

Here's the answer: We get anxious, worried, stressed, confused, and depressed about the situations we are facing. Get down to praying and rehearsing what God has done. You will come out of the prayer time realizing that the God you serve can and will bring you through this as well. Confusion is cleared up when we get a better view of God. Clarification for your situation comes when you have a clear view of Whom you serve. You serve the Almighty God! Nothing is too hard for Him. With God *all* things are possible.

Points to Ponder

1. What do you know about God?

2. Notice in the Scriptures the places where Jeremiah is giving praise in his prayer.

3. If God has these attributes, then is anything too hard for Him? See list below.

Incomparable – 2 Samuel 7:22

Invisible – Isaiah 40:28
Unchangeable – Numbers 23:19
Unequaled – Isaiah 40:13–25
Unsearchable – Romans 11:33-34
Infinite – 1 Kings 8:27
Eternal – Isaiah 57:15
Omnipotence – Jeremiah 32:17-27
Omnipresence – Psalms 139:7–12
Omniscience – 1 John 3:20
Fore-knowledge – Isaiah 48:3-5
Wise – Acts 15:18

35 *A Prayer to Not Miss Our Moment*

Daniel 9:2-19

"During the first year of his reign, I, Daniel, learned from reading the word of the LORD, as revealed to Jeremiah the prophet, that Jerusalem must lie desolate for seventy years.

"So I turned to the Lord God and pleaded with him in prayer and fasting. I also wore rough burlap and sprinkled myself with ashes.

"I prayed to the LORD my God and confessed: 'O Lord, you are a great and awesome God! You always fulfill your covenant and keep your promises of unfailing love to those who love you and obey your commands.

'But we have sinned and done wrong. We have rebelled against you and scorned your commands and regulations.

'We have refused to listen to your servants the prophets, who spoke on your authority to our kings and princes and ancestors and to all the people of the land.

'Lord, you are in the right; but as you see, our faces are covered with shame. This is true of all of us, including the people of Judah and Jerusalem and all Israel, scattered near and far, wherever you have driven us because of our disloyalty to you.

'O LORD, we and our kings, princes, and ancestors are covered with shame because we have sinned against you.

'But the Lord our God is merciful and forgiving, even though we have rebelled against him.

'We have not obeyed the LORD our God, for we have not followed the instructions he gave us through his servants the prophets.

'All Israel has disobeyed your instruction and turned away, refusing to listen to your voice. So now the solemn curses and judgments written in the Law of Moses, the servant of God, have been poured down on us because of our sin.

'You have kept your word and done to us and our rulers exactly as you warned. Never has there been such a disaster as happened in Jerusalem.

'Every curse written against us in the Law of Moses has come true. Yet we have refused to seek mercy from the LORD our God by turning from our sins and recognizing his truth.

'Therefore, the LORD has brought upon us the disaster he prepared. The LORD our God was right to do

Unrestrained

all of these things, for we did not obey him.

'O Lord our God, you brought lasting honor to your name by rescuing your people from Egypt in a great display of power. But we have sinned and are full of wickedness.

'In view of all your faithful mercies, Lord, please turn your furious anger away from your city Jerusalem, your holy mountain. All the neighboring nations mock Jerusalem and your people because of our sins and the sins of our ancestors.

'O our God, hear your servant's prayer! Listen as I plead. For your own sake, Lord, smile again on your desolate sanctuary.

'O my God, lean down and listen to me. Open your eyes and see our despair. See how your city—the city that bears your name—lies in ruins. We make this plea, not because we deserve help, but because of your mercy.

'O Lord, hear. O Lord, forgive. O Lord, listen and act! For your own sake, do not delay, O my God, for your people and your city bear your name.'"

~

Have you ever read a portion of Scripture and it caused you to pray? I have heard and read so many passages of Scripture throughout my years. They were impactful then but even more so now.

I see the world and the changes that have happened so rapidly. Then I read God's Word and I see the truth of His Word even more profoundly. It stirs my heart to say,

"Lord, we need You *now*! We've always needed You, but now we *desperately* need you!"

This is exactly what happened with Daniel. As he studied, through his reading he noticed the timing of his generation. Jeremiah had declared that for seventy years the Hebrews would be in captivity. Daniel did the math and recognized that his generation was on the precipice of liberation!

Can you see the timing of our generation? Do you recognize the season we are in right now? We are on the precipice! We are literally living out the Bible. As you read and study, like Daniel, this ought to cause you to pray.

Daniel said, "[I saw this, and] I turned to the Lord… in prayer and fasting," (vs. 2).

May we turn to the Lord in prayer and fasting and intercede for our nation, families, and friends.

You are a chosen generation. You've been chosen to be a part of this time. Look around! See the timing of our generation and let's be the Daniels of our day. Let us pray that this generation does not miss its moment of liberation! I pray that they won't miss their moment of liberation and you won't miss your moment of intercession either.

Points to Ponder

1. Has there been a time where you felt you

missed your moment? If so, what guidelines have you put into your life to help you not miss these moments?

2. As you read, study, and watch are you seeing the timing of our generation?

3. Have you ever been in intercessory prayer?

For Further Study see Ephesians 6:18; Philippians 1:19; 2 Corinthians 1:11; 1 Timothy 2:1

36 A Prayer of Desperation

Habakkuk 3:1-19

Habakkuk's Prayer
This prayer was sung by the prophet Habakkuk:
"I have heard all about you, LORD. I am filled with awe by your amazing works. In this time of our deep need, help us again as you did in years gone by. And in your anger,
remember your mercy.
"I see God moving across the deserts from Edom, the Holy One coming from Mount Paran. His brilliant splendor fills the heavens, and the earth is filled with his praise.
"His coming is as brilliant as the sunrise. Rays of light flash from his hands, where his awesome power is hidden.
"Pestilence marches before him; plague follows

close behind.

"When he stops, the earth shakes. When he looks, the nations tremble. He shatters the everlasting mountains and levels the eternal hills. He is the Eternal One!

"I see the people of Cushan in distress, and the nation of Midian trembling in terror.

"Was it in anger, LORD, that you struck the rivers and parted the sea? Were you displeased with them? No, you were sending your chariots of salvation!

"You brandished your bow and your quiver of arrows. You split open the earth with flowing rivers.

"The mountains watched and trembled. Onward swept the raging waters. The mighty deep cried out, lifting its hands in submission.

"The sun and moon stood still in the sky as your brilliant arrows flew and your glittering spear flashed.

"You marched across the land in anger and trampled the nations in your fury.

"You went out to rescue your chosen people, to save your anointed ones. You crushed the heads of the wicked and stripped their bones from head to toe.

"With his own weapons, you destroyed the chief of those who rushed out like a whirlwind,

thinking Israel would be easy prey.

"You trampled the sea with your horses, and the mighty waters piled high.

"I trembled inside when I heard this; my lips quivered with fear. My legs gave way beneath me, and I shook in terror. I will wait quietly for the coming day when disaster will strike the people who invade us.

"Even though the fig trees have no blossoms, and there are no grapes on the vines; even though the olive crop fails, and the fields lie empty and barren; even though the flocks die in the fields, and the cattle barns are empty,

"yet I will rejoice in the LORD! I will be joyful in the God of my salvation!

"The Sovereign LORD is my strength! He makes me as surefooted as a deer, able to tread upon the heights."

~

Oftentimes, we are driven to prayer through the extreme pressures that come upon us. We are driven to pray through circumstances that are beyond our control. Many times, these are times of serious emotional and mental pressure. We just begin to pray so that God will relieve the pressure. We pour out our hearts and emotions without much care of what the world around us may think.

These moments of prayer bring a refreshing to our soul and spirits. Even for just the time which we engaged in that prayer we find relief from the pressure.

Habakkuk was under severe pressure. When you read that first verse, the Hebrew gives or adds a word to let us know the style or environment in which it was prayed.

The Hebrew word given is, *Shigionoth*. It's a type of

music with impassioned staccato and quick changes of rhythm and emotion (see Psalms 7: title, note). The root of Shigionoth, *sagah* (Heb.), depicts the movement of a drunken man and is used in this passage to recognize Habakkuk's strong emotional pressure.

You can see then this prayer is one strong emotion. He's praying like a drunken man. He's desperate and needs the Lord to intervene in the situation. Maybe you're there right now. You've experienced so much pressure there's nowhere else to turn. Turn towards God and let all that emotion spring forth out of you.

Look at how Habakkuk did it:

"I have heard all about you, Lord. I am filled with awe by your amazing works. In this time of our deep need, help us again as you did in years gone by. And in your anger, remember your mercy." – Habakkuk 3:2 NLT

In our time of deep need, in this moment of extreme pressure, *Lord, I surely need you now!*

Points to Ponder

1. Turn towards God and let all that emotion spring forth out of you! In your time of deep need, let your prayers be filled with awe and desperation, asking for His intervention just like Habakkuk did.

2. Experience the refreshing relief from pressure that comes from pouring your heart and emotions out in prayer. Take a moment to engage in prayer, finding solace and strength in God's presence.

3. When you're feeling overwhelmed and there's nowhere else to turn, remember that the Lord is always there to help you in your deep need. Just like Habakkuk, ask for His mercy and guidance in the midst of your intense emotions and pressures.

37 Our Prayer

Matthew 6:5-15

"When you pray, don't be like the hypocrites who love to pray publicly on street corners and in the synagogues where everyone can see them. I tell you the truth, that is all the reward they will ever get.

"But when you pray, go away by yourself, shut the door behind you, and pray to your Father in private. Then your Father, who sees everything, will reward you.

"When you pray, don't babble on and on as the Gentiles do. They think their prayers are answered merely by repeating their words again and again.

"Don't be like them, for your Father knows exactly what you need even before you ask him!

"Pray like this:

Our Father in heaven, may your name be kept holy.

"May your Kingdom come soon. May your will be done on earth, as it is in heaven.

"Give us today the food we need,

"and forgive us our sins, as we have forgiven those who sin against us.

"And don't let us yield to temptation, but rescue us from the evil one.

"If you forgive those who sin against you, your heavenly Father will forgive you.

"But if you refuse to forgive others, your Father will not forgive your sins."

~

The *Sermon on the Mount* is a teaching discourse by Jesus. He taught so many profound and yet simple godly principles in this sermon. Through this discourse or sermon, Jesus teaches them as well as us the principle of prayer.

He simply says *when you pray, here's how you do it.*

1. Seek God not man!

The Pharisees gathered three times a day to pray in the synagogue or the temple. Although, the Pharisees weren't gathering to pray to seek the Lord, but to be seen by man. On the way to these scheduled times of prayer, they would stop along the street and begin to pray loudly and overtly expressing themselves so that people would say, "Would look at how spiritual they are!"

We see people do this subtly even now. They will post, "The Lord woke me up at three this morning, and the He spoke to me." We desire to let people know that we are spiritual. Jesus said *don't do that, that's hypocrisy.*

2. *Simple prayers are effective prayers.*

A short concise prayer is as powerful as a long drawn-out prayer. In Ecclesiastes 5:2, Solomon stated, "God is in heaven, you are on earth, therefore let your words be few." Oftentimes we believe the longer we prayer the more God hears. Jesus said, *they think that they shall be heard for their many words.* Just simply connect with God and talk with him in your own way.

3. *Set your mind on God!*

We can be guilty of going through the motions, singing the words, and even repeating the words of this prayer, without thinking about God. Jesus called that meaningless repetition. Jesus didn't say that repetition is wrong, meaningless repetition is wrong. Jesus himself repeated prayers. In Matthew 26 Jesus makes the same request three times. Engage your mind and pray with a sensitive heart to God.

Even if you repeat the words of this sample prayer Jesus gave to us, if you pray it with a mind set upon God, this is a powerful, potent, and perfect prayer.

Points to Ponder

1. Start with Praise. *Hallowed be Your name!* Give honor and respect to Whom you are addressing in your prayer.

2. Seek provision from God. *Give us our daily bread.*

3. Safety and protection are afforded to you by God. *Deliver us from evil.*

Sum it all up with praise. *For thine is the kingdom, and the power, and the glory, forever. Amen!*

38 *I Pray for You*

John 17:1-26

"After saying all these things, Jesus looked up to heaven and said, 'Father, the hour has come. Glorify your Son so he can give glory back to you.

'For you have given him authority over everyone. He gives eternal life to each one you have given him.

'And this is the way to have eternal life—to know you, the only true God, and Jesus Christ, the one you sent to earth.

'I brought glory to you here on earth by completing the work you gave me to do.

'Now, Father, bring me into the glory we shared before the world began.

'I have revealed you to the ones you gave me from this world. They were always yours. You gave them to me, and they have kept your word.

'Now they know that everything I have is a gift from you,

'for I have passed on to them the message you gave me. They accepted it and know that I came from you, and they believe you sent me.

'My prayer is not for the world, but for those you have given me, because they belong to you.

'All who are mine belong to you, and you have given them to me, so they bring me glory.

'Now I am departing from the world; they are staying in this world, but I am coming to you. Holy Father, you have given me your name; now protect them by the power of your name so that they will be united just as we are.

'During my time here, I protected them by the power of the name you gave me. I guarded them so that not one was lost, except the one headed for destruction, as the Scriptures foretold.

'Now I am coming to you. I told them many things while I was with them in this world so they would be filled with my joy.

'I have given them your word. And the world hates them because they do not belong to the world, just as I do not belong to the world.

'I'm not asking you to take them out of the world, but to keep them safe from the evil one.

'They do not belong to this world any more than I do.

'Make them holy by your truth; teach them your

word, which is truth.

'Just as you sent me into the world, I am sending them into the world.

'And I give myself as a holy sacrifice for them so they can be made holy by your truth.

'I am praying not only for these disciples but also for all who will ever believe in me through their message.

'I pray that they will all be one, just as you and I are one—as you are in me, Father, and I am in you. And may they be in us so that the world will believe you sent me.

'I have given them the glory you gave me, so they may be one as we are one.

'I am in them and you are in me. May they experience such perfect unity that the world will know that you sent me and that you love them as much as you love me.

'Father, I want these whom you have given me to be with me where I am. Then they can see all the glory you gave me because you loved me even before the world began!

'O righteous Father, the world doesn't know you, but I do; and these disciples know you sent me.

'I have revealed you to them, and I will continue to do so. Then your love for me will be in them, and I will be in them.'"

~

If you were to ask me about the Lord's Prayer, I

would guide you to this prayer more than the model prayer that Jesus prayed in Matthew 6. In Mathew 6, Jesus was instructing on how to pray. Here where Jesus prays, He prayed for his disciples. He prayed for those who were currently his disciples and then prayed for those who would become His disciples.

Jesus had been speaking directly to those around Him, but now He is praying to the Heavenly Father. Jesus prays for unity and truth. We must be able to speak truth and still maintain unity. Today there's much "truth" but it's dividing. At times, truth will certainly cause division. However, when we speak truth it should be done in love. Ephesians 4:15 gives that directive. We should speak truth in love. Remember that love without truth is hypocrisy and truth without love it brutality. Unity is kept by telling or speaking truth in absolute love. While it may not be easy it is absolutely necessary.

Jesus then prays about the giving of the glory. Jesus said *I have given them the glory*. All of them received the glory. Yes, even the ones who would deny Him and the ones who would betray Him; they received as well. That glory also extends to you!

Romans 8:30 states it like this:

"And having chosen them, he called them to come to him. And having called them, he gave them right standing with himself. And having given them right standing, he gave them his glory."

Think about that. The Lord looks at us not in our state of denial or in our state of betrayal. He sees us in the glorified state. You have been chosen, justified, and you are glorified. If we looked at each other the way God looks at us, we would be a unified people. Wouldn't it be amazing if we saw the glory in each other? Think about the people who get on your nerves the most. Then think about how God views them.

Someone once stated, *"love is blind, marriage is an eye opener."* The reality is that love isn't blind, it's just able to see more, and because love sees more it is willing to see less. We should pray more and then we would see less. Praying for others creates a love for them and brings us into unity as the body.

May we see each other and ourselves as God sees us!

Points to Ponder

1. Do you pray for others as Jesus prayed for them? Using the model here in John 17 begin praying for others as Jesus did!

2. Have you ever witnessed disunity because of truth spoken without love?

Have you prayed for those who annoy you and bother you? Ask the Lord to show you how He views them?

39 Praying Bold Prayers

Acts 4:23-31

"As soon as they were freed, Peter and John returned to the other believers and told them what the leading priests and elders had said.

"When they heard the report, all the believers lifted their voices together in prayer to God: 'O Sovereign Lord, Creator of heaven and earth, the sea, and everything in them—

'you spoke long ago by the Holy Spirit through our ancestor David, your servant, saying,

'Why were the nations so angry? Why did they waste their time with futile plans?

'The kings of the earth prepared for battle; the rulers gathered together against the LORD

and against his Messiah.'

'In fact, this has happened here in this very city! For

Unrestrained

Herod Antipas, Pontius Pilate the governor, the Gentiles, and the people of Israel were all united against Jesus, your holy servant, whom you anointed.

'But everything they did was determined beforehand according to your will.

'And now, O Lord, hear their threats, and give us, your servants, great boldness in preaching your word.

'Stretch out your hand with healing power; may miraculous signs and wonders be done through the name of your holy servant Jesus.'

"After this prayer, the meeting place shook, and they were all filled with the Holy Spirit. Then they preached the word of God with boldness."

~

The setting of the prayer here actually begins in Acts 3 and verse 1. Peter and John were on their way to the temple to pray. As they headed for prayer, they encountered a lame man laying by the gate. From the lame man's perspective, I am sure he was thankful that Peter and John were willing to stop and give him attention. I'm sure that during the prayer service, they would have, as I often do in my prayer, asked for God to send His power and perform great miracles. Yet how often do we walk by the very opportunities for that prayer to be performed in our lives? More often than not, opportunity looks and feels like distraction and derailment of and from our plans.

What I find so interesting in that scene of Acts 3 is

what I would say is believers acting in boldness. A man asks expecting silver or gold. The disciples say *we don't have silver and gold, but what we do have is what you really need anyway.* Try that the next time you see someone laying or sitting along the sidewalk begging. I think you would spend more than a few minutes of pause! Why? It takes boldness to do what Peter and John did that day.

Do you have that kind of boldness? After all this the disciples prayed that they would be granted boldness to speak His Word.

As you read this story it's a harbinger of today. As they showed boldness there was intimidation, threat, imprisonment, and false charges. Instead of backing down, they instead prayed for boldness.

The more you are threatened, intimidated, falsely accused, or the enemy tries to silence you, the more boldness you will need. Peter and John were bold and then asked for more boldness. You must be bold to obey God and do the will of God for your life.

Pray for boldness and then be as bold as lions!

Points to Ponder

1. Acts 25-27 are a fulfillment of the Messianic Prophecies in Psalm 2. Opposition to Jesus and the will of God was fulfilling a prophecy. Have you thought opposition was a sign you were on the right track?

2. In asking for boldness, you are recognizing that if you will do your part, God will certainly do His part. In that you are pleasing to God, for without faith it is impossible to please Him.

3. Acts 4:31 says that there was a physical manifestation of the Power of God at the conclusion of the prayer service. Read Ephesians 5:18; Acts 2:4; 4:8; 4:31; 9:17; and 13:9. Why is it so important to be filled with His Spirit?

40 Praying for Those Who are Doing Well

Ephesians 1:15-23 and 3:14-21

"Ever since I first heard of your strong faith in the Lord Jesus and your love for God's people everywhere,

"I have not stopped thanking God for you. I pray for you constantly,

"asking God, the glorious Father of our Lord Jesus Christ, to give you spiritual wisdom and insight so that you might grow in your knowledge of God.

"I pray that your hearts will be flooded with light so that you can understand the confident hope he has given to those he called—his holy people who are his rich and glorious inheritance.

"I also pray that you will understand the incredible greatness of God's power for us who believe him. This is the same mighty power "that raised Christ from the dead and seated him in the place of honor at God's right hand in the heavenly realms.

"Now he is far above any ruler or authority or power or leader or anything else—not only in this world but also in the world to come.

"God has put all things under the authority of Christ and has made him head over all things for the benefit of the church.

"And the church is his body; it is made full and complete by Christ, who fills all things everywhere with himself."

Ephesians 3:14-21

"When I think of all this, I fall to my knees and pray to the Father,

"the Creator of everything in heaven and on earth.

"I pray that from his glorious, unlimited resources he will empower you with inner strength through his Spirit.

"Then Christ will make his home in your hearts as you trust in him. Your roots will grow down into God's love and keep you strong.

"And may you have the power to understand, as all God's people should, how wide, how long, how high, and how deep his love is.

"May you experience the love of Christ, though it is too great to understand fully. Then you will be made complete with all the fullness of life and power that comes from God.

"Now all glory to God, who is able, through his mighty power at work within us, to accomplish infinitely more than we might ask or think.

"Glory to him in the church and in Christ Jesus through all generations forever and ever! Amen."

~

Paul opens the prayer for the church at Ephesus by taking a position of intensity. He says *for this reason I bow my knee*. Taking a knee was to take a position of intensity. Paul was in prison and in that place he was going to pray intensely for those whom he cared for.

He opened the entire letter to the people of the Ephesian church by declaring the magnificent plan God had for them. Then Paul talks to God about the people. He tells *them* about the Lord and then tells the *Lord* about them. Never cease to pray for those whom you have shared the Gospel with. It's one thing to tell them about Jesus, however go to Jesus about them as well. Prayer makes a difference.

Get into that position of intensity for those whom you care about, for those whom you love, and for those with whom you have shared the message and hope of Jesus. Pray for them, declare God's promises over them, and declare freedom and liberty over them. Ask God to give them favor with man and power with Him. Paul doesn't just pray for those who were hurting and facing difficulties. Paul said, *when I heard how well you were doing I prayed for you.*

We need to pray for those who are doing well. We need to wrestle against the powers, principalities, and rulers of darkness because they are certainly planning an attack on those who are doing well. The enemy isn't attacking those who have already succumbed, but he is attacking those who have not yet surrendered.

Pray, fight, and war for those who are fighting a good fight. Pray for the ones who didn't turn in a prayer request. They need someone fighting for them too. Let's all fight a valiant fight of faith for each other.

Points to Ponder

1. Paul prayed that the eyes of their hearts would be open so they would see two things specifically (Ephesians 1:18): The hope of His calling and the riches of His glory of His inheritance in the saints. Are you focused on the hope and richness of God in your life?

2. In Ephesians 3:17 the Word translated "dwell" literally means *settle down and be at home*. Is Christ at home in your own heart? My prayer is that Christ will be settled down and at home in your heart, therefore things will also be settled down for you as well.

3. In Ephesians 3:18 he asks that you know the love

of Christ which passes knowledge; that you be filled with all the fullness of God. How can you know something that passes knowledge? How can you be filled with fullness of God, yet the universe cannot contain Him? To know the height, the depth, length, and width of the Love of God look no further than the cross. To know the fullness of God don't forsake communion with God or the communion table. It is there that you fully partake and understand the fulness of God's love for you.

41 Pray Without Ceasing

Colossians 4:2-4 and 1 Thessalonians 5:17-18

"Devote yourselves to prayer with an alert mind and a thankful heart.

"Pray for us, too, that God will give us many opportunities to speak about his mysterious plan concerning Christ. That is why I am here in chains.

"Pray that I will proclaim this message as clearly as I should."

1 Thessalonians 5:17-18

"Never stop praying.

"Be thankful in all circumstances, for this is God's will for you who belong to Christ Jesus."

~

Paul exhorts us to devote ourselves personally to prayer. We are further instructed to be a people who pray without ceasing. Paul would say to the church in Ephesus that he would not cease to give thanks for them. The Greek idea of *cease not* is the same as *a tickle in the throat*. In other words, Paul would be praying throughout the day as naturally and as spontaneously as if he were clearing a tickle in his throat.

That's how we must be with each other. All of us fight battles that no one even knows about. However, the Holy Spirit is well aware of the battle we all fight. There may be times in which you feel the urge to pray. Please pray. You'll never know what your obedience to that urge can do for the one who is urgently in need of prayer.

Maybe you say, I don't know what to pray. This is exactly why we must be filled with His Spirit.

"And the Holy Spirit helps us in our weakness. For example, we don't know what God wants us to pray for. But the Holy Spirit prays for us with groanings that cannot be expressed in words.

And the Father who knows all hearts knows what the Spirit is saying, for the Spirit pleads for us believers in harmony with God's own will," – Romans 8:26-27, New Living Translation (NLT).

When we don't know how, what, or even the direction our prayer should be aimed, the Spirit of God makes intercession for us. The Spirit knows the will of God and will give your prayer the perfect direction.

We pray because God has chosen prayer as the vehicle by which He works in us, for us, and through us.

Unrestrained

James 4:2 lets us know that if we do not pray, then we can limit what God would and could do, all of which He desires to do if we pray.

Paul prayed a prayer of seven-fold blessing over the Church. I leave you with the same prayer over your life. May God bless you and keep you and may the Lord bless you.

So we have not stopped praying for you since we first heard about you. We ask God to give you complete knowledge of his will and to give you spiritual wisdom and understanding. Then the way you live will always honor and please the Lord, and your lives will produce every kind of good fruit. All the while, you will grow as you learn to know God better and better. We also pray that you will be strengthened with all his glorious power so you will have all the endurance and patience you need. May you be filled with joy, always thanking the Father. He has enabled you to share in the inheritance that belongs to his people, who live in the light. For he has rescued us from the kingdom of darkness and transferred us into the Kingdom of his dear Son, who purchased our freedom and forgave our sins.

– Colossians 1:9-14

May God grant that to you as an answer to my prayer!

42 A Prayer to be Sent

Isaiah 6:1-8

"It was in the year King Uzziah died that I saw the Lord. He was sitting on a lofty throne, and the train of his robe filled the Temple.

"Attending him were mighty seraphim, each having six wings. With two wings they covered their faces, with two they covered their feet, and with two they flew.

"They were calling out to each other, 'Holy, holy, holy is the LORD of Heaven's Armies!

'The whole earth is filled with his glory!'

"Their voices shook the Temple to its foundations, and the entire building was filled with smoke.

"Then I said, 'It's all over! I am doomed, for I am a sinful man. I have filthy lips, and I live among a people with filthy lips. Yet I have seen the King, the LORD of Heaven's Armies.'

"Then one of the seraphim flew to me with a burning coal he had taken from the altar with a pair of tongs.

"He touched my lips with it and said, 'See, this coal has touched your lips. Now your guilt is removed, and your sins are forgiven.'

"Then I heard the Lord asking, 'Whom should I send as a messenger to this people? Who will go for us?' I said, 'Here I am. Send me.'"

~

The year was 739 BC, but considering the conditions, it could have been any given time in our society. Isaiah was a young man who, considering the status of his nation, was restless. The last King who was good had just passed away. The Israelites are now hanging in the balance between prosperity and destruction.

Isaiah is living a righteous life in the present circumstances. Likewise, we are told that we should live righteously and soberly in this present world (Titus 2:12). Isaiah was desperate for there to be a change. Upon seeing the condition of his nation, he felt a longing: First, to become closer to God. Second, he desired to be a solution in the healing and prosperity of his nation. God obliged the requests of Isaiah.

Isaiah had a vision from God. He was able to see the throne room of God. Before we go win or change the world, we must have a vision from the Lord. Remember, the disciples were given the Great Commission, but then were told, *before you go, wait!* They waited in Jerusalem until the Day of Pentecost. Once they were empowered and strengthened, then they went. We cannot go until we are prepared.

God prepared Isaiah. He cleanses him, removes the condemnation, and then calls him. When Isaiah became clean, God asks: "Whom shall I send? Who will go for us?" Isaiah never hesitated, "Lord, here I am, send me!"

I deeply believe that the Church is in a cleansing state. We see the trouble of our nation, and I believe the Lord is calling us to be a part of the solution. Will you pray, "Here I am, send me!"?

When the people of God stop relying on the world systems to change things and realize the only way to tip the scale away from destruction back towards prosperity is when we, the people of God, *GO!*

My prayer is: *Lord, send us and may we answer the call!*

Points to Ponder

1. What are three things that Isaiah saw in his vision of the Lord?

2. Do you see the despair of the people around you and living in this nation?

3. Can you recognize the simultaneous paths of

our nation? As we turned from being a nation that blessed God, God's blessing began to be removed.

4. What can you do, and where can you go to make a difference in our land?

Are you willing to pray, *Lord, send me*?

Endnotes

Message from the Author
2 Chronicles 7:14, New Living Translation
Acts 12, New Living Translation
Psalms 20:5, New Living Translation

Foreword
Psalms 142, New Living Translation
Numbers 6:24-26, New Living Translation

Introduction
Acts 2, New Living Translation
Acts 1:5-8, New Living Translation

Abraham Prays Over Sodom
Genesis 18:20-33, New Living Translation

Jacob's Prayer for Mercy
Genesis 32:6-12, New Living Translation

Moses Prays to Overcome Doubt
Exodus 3:1-22, New Living Translation
Tyndale House Publishers. (2015). Holy Bible: New Living Translation (Heb 10:32). Tyndale House Publishers.

Signs of the LORD's Power
Exodus 4:1-17, New Living Translation

When Prayer Turns to Praise
Exodus 15:1-18, New Living Translation

A Prayer of Intervention
Exodus 32:1-7, 11-14, New Living Translation
1 Peter 5:8, New Living Translation
Moses' Prayer of Repentance
Exodus 32:30-34, New Living Translation
Proverbs 29:18, New Living Translation
Psalms 86, New Living Translation

Praying for God's Presence
Exodus 33:12 – 34:2-9, New Living Translation
Psalms 16:11, New Living Translation
Nehemiah 8:10, New Living Translation
Hebrews 11:25
Romans 5:2

A Prayer During Discouragement
Numbers 11:1-30, New Living Translation

A Prayer Against Rebellion
Numbers 14:10-20, New Living Translation
Numbers 13:33, New Living Translation
Quote from George Cecil, *Brainy Quotes*, www.brainyquotes.com

A 40-Day Prayer
Deuteronomy 9:18-29, New Living Translation

Hebrews 4:16, New Living Translation
1 Corinthians 1:14-15, New Living Translation

Prayer After a Defeat
Joshua 7:2-15, New Living Translation
Matthew 28:19, New Living Translation

Praying for a Child
1 Samuel 1:1-20, New Living Translation

A Prayer of Praise
1 Samuel 2:1-10, New Living Translation
Luke 1:46, New Living Translation

A Kingdom-Minded Prayer
2 Samuel 7:18-29, New Living Translation
Ephesians 3:18-20, New Living Translation
Acts 2:29-30, New Living Translation

Praising for Deliverance
2 Samuel 22:1-7, New Living Translation
2 Samuel 22:26-32, New Living Translation
2 Samuel 22:50, New Living Translation
2 Samuel 22:21-25, New Living Translation
Psalms 38, New Living Translation
Psalms 51, New Living Translation
Psalms 18, New Living Translation
Romans 15:9, New Living Translation

Praying for Wisdom
1 Kings 3:3-15, New Living Translation

Ecclesiastes 1:12-18, New Living Translation

A Prayer of Dedication
1 Kings 8:22-26, New Living Translation
1 Kings 8:54-61, New Living Translation
1 Kings 6, New Living Translation
1 Kings 7, New Living Translation
1 Corinthians 3:16, King James Version
John 3:16, King James Version
Ephesians 2:10, New Living Translation

A Prayer of Dejection
1 Kings 19:9-18, New Living Translation

A Prayer Out of Distress
2 Kings 19:14-19, New Living Translation

A Prayer for Healing
2 Kings 20:1-11, New Living Translation
A Prayer of Thankfulness
1 Chronicles 17:16-27, New Living Translation
2 Samuel 18:7, New Living Translation

A Prayer for Cheerfulness in Giving
1 Chronicles 19:10-20, New Living Translation
2 Corinthians 9:7, English Standard Version
Quote from Jim Elliott, *The Journals of Jim Elliot*, © 1978 Elisabeth Elliot, Published by Fleming H. Revell a division of Baker Book House Company
1 Chronicles 29:3-5, New Living Translation

A Prayer Motivated by Fear
2 Chronicles 20:1-23, New Living Translation
2 Chronicles 20:9, New Living Translation

Praying for a Nation
Ezra 9:1 – 10:4, New Living Translation
Exodus 34:12-16, New Living Translation
Deuteronomy 7:3-5, New Living Translation

Begin With Prayer
Nehemiah 1:3-11, New Living Translation
Quote from R. T. Kendall,
Philippians 4:6-7, New King James Version
Proverbs 19:21, New Living Translation

Praying When Life Gets Overwhelming
Psalms 3:1-8, New Living Translation
John 10:10, New Living Translation
Ephesians 6:13-14, New Living Translation
Psalms 46:1-3, New Living Translation
Psalms 37, New Living Translation

Turning Your Prayer into Praise
Psalms 8:1-9, New Living Translation
Exodus 25 – 39, New Living Translation
Psalms 22:22, New Living Translation
Hebrews 2:11-12, New Living Translation
Exodus 28:7-8, New Living Translation

Psalms 8:1, 3-4, 9, New King James Version
Psalms 8:2, New King James Version
Matthew 21, New Living Translation

A Prayer for a Clean Heart
Psalms 19:1-14, New Living Translation
Psalms 19:7, New King James Version
Psalms 19:8, New Living Translation
Ephesians 5:26, New Living Translation
Psalms 19:14, New Living Translation
Psalms 119, New Living Translation

The 23rd Psalm
Psalms 23:1-6, New Living Translation

A Prayer of Forgiveness
Psalms 51:1-19, New Living Translation
Psalms 139:23-24, New Living Translation
Psalms 51, New Living Translation
Genesis 1:1, New Living Translation

A Prayer for Guidance and Understanding
Psalms 139:1-24, New Living Translation
Matthew 12:37, New Living Translation
Psalms 139:13-16, New Living Translation
Judges 3, New Living Translation

A Prayer for His Presence
Isaiah 64:1-9, New Living Translation
Psalms 37, New Living Translation

1 Corinthians 2:9, King James Version
Isaiah 64:1-4, New Living Translation
James 4:2, King James Version
Psalms 37:4, New Living Translation
Further Study
Ephesians 3:20
Psalms 16:11
James 4:2
Matthew 7:7

A Prayer for Clarification
Jeremiah 32:16-27, New Living Translation
2 Samuel 7:22, New Living Translation
Isaiah 40:28, New Living Translation
Numbers 23:19, New Living Translation
Isaiah 40:13-25, New Living Translation
Romans 11:33-34, New Living Translation
1 Kings 8:27, New Living Translation
Isaiah 57:15, New Living Translation
Jeremiah 32:17-27, New Living Translation
Psalms 139:7-12, New Living Translation
1 John 3:20, New Living Translation
Isaiah 48:3-5, New Living Translation
Acts 15:18, New Living Translation

A Prayer to Not Miss Our Moment
Daniel 9:2-19, New Living Translation
Further Study
Ephesians 6:18
Philippians 1:19

2 Corinthians 1:11
1 Timothy 2:1

A Prayer of Desperation
Habakkuk 3:1-19, New Living Translation
Psalms 7, New Living Translation

Our Prayer
Matthew 6:5-15, New Living Translation
Ecclesiastes 5:2, New Living Translation

I Pray for You
John 17:1-26, New Living Translation
Matthew 6, New Living Translation
Ephesians 4:15, New Living Translation
Romans 8:30, New Living Translation

Praying Bold Prayers
Acts 4:23-31, New Living Translation
Acts 3:1, New Living Translation
Acts 22 – 27, New Living Translation
Psalms 2, New Living Translation
Acts 4:31, New Living Translation
Ephesians 5:18, New Living Translation
Acts 2:4, 4:8, 4:31, 9:17, 13:9, New Living Translation

Praying for Those Who Are Doing Well
Ephesians 1:15-23, New Living Translation
Ephesians 3:14-21, New Living Translation
Ephesians 1:18, New Living Translation

Ephesians 3:17, New Living Translation
Ephesians 3:18, New Living Translation

Pray Without Ceasing
Colossians 4:2, New Living Translation
1 Thessalonians 5:17, New Living Translation
Romans 8:26-27, New Living Translation
James 4:2, New Living Translation
Colossians 1:9-14, New Living Translation

A Prayer to be Sent
Isaiah 6:1-8, New Living Translation
Titus 2:12, New Living Translation

About the Author

Jason McKinnies is a man of profound influence and inspiration. His life's mission revolves around the art of leaving a lasting legacy. As a renowned Senior Pastor, visionary leader, and successful entrepreneur, Jason has dedicated his life to empowering others to discover their purpose and make a positive impact on the world.

With an impressive background in ministry and business, Jason serves as the Senior Pastor of Purpose House Church in Herrin, Illinois, where he provides steadfast oversight, guiding its direction and vision. Under his compassionate leadership, Purpose House Church has grown into a thriving community, empowering individuals to find and embrace their unique calling.

Beyond his pastoral role, Jason serves as a director for Farmers State Bank and as the Chief

Executive Officer for FSB Insurance, a subsidiary of Farmers State Bank.

With his charismatic speaking style and relatable stories, Jason captivates audiences, encouraging them to envision the impact they can make in their communities, families. Businesses and beyond. His authenticity radiates through his words, inspiring listeners to embrace their uniqueness, step into their potential, and leave a lasting mark on the world for Jesus Christ.

Jason resides in Southern Illinois with his wife of more than twenty years, and ministry partner, Melissa. Together they have two daughters, Morgan and Zoe.

Milton Keynes UK
Ingram Content Group UK Ltd.
UKHW031020011224
451693UK00004B/597